MANDARIN CHINESE

Phrase Book & Dictionary

Kan Qian

Language consultant: Kan Jia

BBC Active, an imprint of Educational Publishers LLP, part of the Pearson Education Group, Edinburgh Gate, Harlow, Essex CM20 2JE, England

First published 2007
Fourth impression 2010

ISBN 978-1-4066-1210-3

Cover design: Two Associates
Cover photograph: VStock/Alamy
Insides design: Pentacor book design
Layout: Rob Lian and Lucy Appleby
Illustrations © Joanna Kerr, New Division
Series editor: Philippa Goodrich
Development manager: Tara Dempsey
Senior production controller: Man Fai Lau

Printed and bound in China. CTPSC/04

how to use this book

This book is divided into colour-coded sections to help you find the language you need as quickly as possible. You can also refer to the **contents** on pages 4–5, and the contents lists at the start of each section.

Along with travel and language tips, each section contains:

YOU MAY WANT TO SAY... language you'll need for every situation

YOU MAY SEE... words and phrases you'll see on signs or in print

YOU MAY HEAR... questions, instructions or information people may ask or give you

On page 16 you'll find **essentials**, a list of basic, all-purpose phrases to help you start communicating straight away.

Many of the phrases can be adapted by simply using another word from the dictionary. For instance, take the question 飞机场在哪儿? *fēijīchǎng zài nǎr* (Where is the airport?), if you want to know where the station is, just substitute 车站 *chēzhàn* (station) for 飞机场 *fēijīchǎng* to give 车站在哪儿? *chēzhàn zài nǎr*.

The **pronunciation guide** is based on English sounds, and is explained on page 6. If you want to find out about Chinese characters, see page 12. If you want some guidance on how the Chinese language works, see **basic grammar** on page 167. The **dictionary** is separated into two sections: English–Chinese (page 173) and Chinese–English (page 211).

We welcome any comments or suggestions about this book, but in the meantime, have a good trip – 一路顺风! *yīlù shùnfēng*

contents

pronunciation guide

The official Chinese language is the language of Han Chinese, the largest ethnic group in China. Hence it is called hanyu (*lit.* Han language). It is also known as zhongwen and zhongguohua. In Taiwan, Hong Kong, and other overseas Chinese communities it is also referred to as guoyu or huayu. The spoken Chinese varies from province to province, and even from village to village. For example, Cantonese is one of the eight major dialects. These dialects share the same written language but differ immensely in pronunciation. There is a modern standard form of the spoken language which is spoken and understood by the majority of the population. This standard form is known as putonghua (*lit.* common speech) in mainland China, and as 'Mandarin Chinese' in English-speaking countries. Putonghua (Mandarin Chinese) is based on the pronunciation of the Beijing dialect. The term 'Chinese' in this book means Mandarin Chinese or putonghua.

Pinyin is the official system adopted in the People's Republic of China in 1958 to transcribe Chinese sounds into the Latin script. Pinyin is now adopted almost universally for transliterating Chinese personal names and place names (e.g. Peking was the old spelling and Beijing is the pinyin spelling). The transliteration system used in this book is pinyin.

The majority of Chinese words are made up of one or two syllables. A syllable may consist of a single vowel, a compound vowel (e.g. ou, ei, ing) or a vowel preceded by a consonant. Sounds that appear before vowels are called 'initials' (like 'consonants' in English) and the remaining sounds are called 'finals' (ie vowels and vowels with a nasal sound). Each syllable is represented by a Chinese character.

Compared with some other languages, Chinese has fewer sounds, 23 initials and 34 finals (if you count the variants of e and i, there are 36). Many of those sounds bear some resemblance to English sounds. There are only a handful of Chinese sounds which are peculiar to Western ears. Don't be discouraged by them.

* initials

LETTER	APPROX ENGLISH EQUIVALENT
f, l, m, n, s, w, y	similar to English
p, t, k	like *p* in *poor*, *t* in *tar* and *k* in *kite*
b, d	(more abrupt than their English equivalents) like *p* in *spend*, and *t* in *stamp*
g	like *g* in *girl*
h	like *h* in *hole* (but with a little friction in the throat)
j	like *g* in *George* (but with the tongue nearer the teeth)
q	a bit like *ch* in *cheese* (but with the tongue further forward)
z	like *ds* in *loads*
c	like *ts* in *toasts*
r	a bit like *r* in *run* (but with the tongue loosely rolled in the middle of the mouth)

zh	like *j* in *jail* (but with the tongue further back)
ch	a bit like *ch* in *chair* (but with the tongue further back and the mouth in a round shape)
sh	like *sh* in *short*
x	a bit like *sh* in *sheep* (the front of the tongue lies behind the lower front teeth, the tongue is in a relaxed manner, and the mouth is at its natural shape, now try to whistle)

* finals

LETTER	APPROX ENGLISH EQUIVALENT
a	like *a* in *father*
ai	like *igh* in *high* (but with a narrower mouth shape)
ao	like *ow* in *how*
an	like *an* in *ban*
ang	like *on* in *monster*
e	like *ur* in *fur*
ei	like *ay* in *bay*
en	like *en* in *tent*
eng	en plus the strong nasal sound, a bit like *un* in *hunger*
er	*ur* in *fur* (with the tongue rolled back)
i	like *ea* in *tea* (but when i is preceded by z, c, s, zh, ch, sh and r, it simply functions as a helper to make those sounds audible)

ia	combine i and a
iao	like *eow* in *meow*
ie	like *ye* in *yes*
iu	like *you*
ian	similar to the Japanese currency word *yen*
in	like *in* in *bin*
iang	like *young*
	like *ing* in *outing*
iong	combine i with ong
o	like *ore* in *more*
ou	like *oa* in *toast*
ong	a bit like *ong* in *ding-dong*
u	like *oo* in *boot*
ua	combine u with a
uo	like *war*
uai	combine u with ai
ui	like *wai* in *waiting*
uan	like *one*
un	a bit like *won* in *wonder*
uang	like *wan* in *wanting*
ü	like the French *u* in *tu*
üe	combine ü with a short ei
üan	combine ü with a short an
ün	a bit like *une* in French

When initials do not precede u at the beginning of a syllable, w replaces u, e.g. wang instead of uang, wo instead of uo.

When ü follows j, q, x and y, it is written as u without the two dots over it but still pronounced as ü because u never occurs after these initials, e.g. ju and qu, not jü and qü.

The apostrophe is used to separate two syllables whenever there may be confusion over the syllable boundary. For example in chang'an (long peace), g belongs to the first syllable not the second.

* tones

Every syllable in isolation is given a specific tone which helps to distinguish the meaning. Many words with exactly the same pronunciation but different tones mean completely different things. For example, tang in its high-level tone means 'soup' (汤), while in its rising tone means 'sugar'(糖). Don't be put off by this, even if you use the wrong tone, the context, your facial expression and many other things will always help to put the message across.

In putonghua (Mandarin) there are four basic tones:

		TONE MARK
The first tone	(high-level)	ˉ
The second tone	(rising)	ˊ
The third tone	(falling-rising)	ˇ
The fourth tone	(falling)	ˋ

In terms of an average person's voice range, the four tones can be visually represented like this:

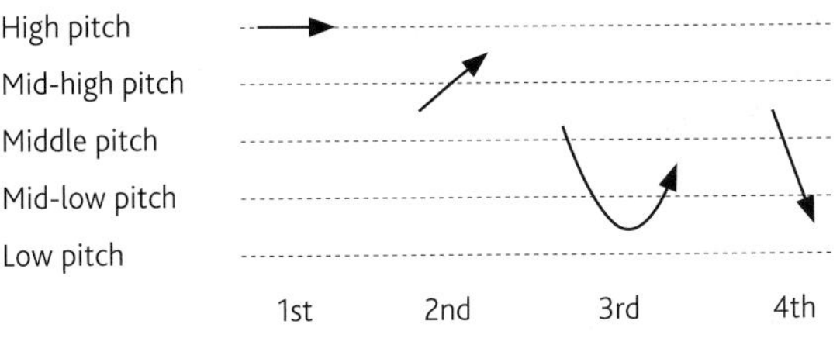

In addition to the above four basic tones, there is a neutral tone. Syllables with neutral tones are pronounced very weakly. If there is no tone mark over the vowel, the syllable must be a neutral tone. For example:

mā	*má*	*mǎ*	*mà*	*ma*
妈	麻	马	骂	吗
mother	linen	horse	to swear	question word

Tones do change as a result of other tones surrounding them. The three most common changes are:

i) When two third tones are together in the same meaning group, the first third tone usually changes to the second tone, e.g. nǐ, hǎo → Ní hǎo (hello).

ii) When bù (not) is followed by another fourth tone, it changes to the second tone, e.g. bú shì (no).

iii) The number word yī (one) has the first tone when used in isolation or at the end of a word or phrase, e.g. yī (one) and shí'yī (eleven); yī changes to the second tone when preceding fourth tones, e.g. yí liàng chē (one car); and yī changes to the fourth tone when preceding all the other three tones, e.g. yì běn shū (one book), yì jīn píngguǒ (one *jin* of apples), yì tóu niú (one cow). However, some people do use the first tone for yi all the time.

In this book, all the words in pinyin are marked with tones as if each syllable were in isolation. For example, the phrase nǐ hǎo is marked with two third tones, which does not reflect the tone change. The only exception is bù (not). It is always marked with the second tone when followed by a fourth tone, e.g. bú shì (no).

* understanding Chinese characters

Written Chinese is believed to be among the world's oldest written languages. Many of the earliest writings looked like pictures, known as pictographs. Gradually, the picture-like symbols have evolved into characters formed of strokes, and the structures have become more systemized and simpler. For example, the character for 'the sun' used to look like this: ⊙, and now it looks like this: 日.

There are about 50,000 Chinese characters, of which 3,000 are used for everyday purposes. There is no correlation between how characters are pronounced and how they are written. If you can read characters, the tones become much less important in distinguishing the meaning.

A stroke is a single unbroken line. There are some basic strokes on which many other combinations are based. They are:

STROKES

一	horizontal stroke – from left to right
丨	vertical stroke – from top to bottom
ノ	left-falling dot – from right to bottom left
丶	right-falling dot – from left to bottom right
丿	left-falling – from top right to bottom left
㇏	right-falling – from top left to bottom right
㇀	rising – from bottom left to top right
亅乚	hook – all downward first, then make a hook
㇇㇆	turning – all from left to right first, then make a turning

In writing a character, you are supposed to follow the following rules regarding stroke order:

- horizontal stroke, then vertical
- left, then right
- top, then bottom
- outside, then inside
- partly outside, then inside, then close
- middle, then left, then right

The majority of the Chinese characters consists of two main parts – one can be called the category headword (also known as 'radical') which indicates the categorization of characters and the other is called the 'phonetic' which provides some clue to the pronunciation. For example, the character 清, pronounced *qīng* (meaning 'pure, clear'), consists of two components: the left is called the 'water headword', and the the right part gives the pronunciation *qing*.

You need to remember each headword and how to write it first, and you also need to know how the other part is pronounced before it can function as a phonetic.

HEADWORD	ENGLISH	NAME IN PINYIN
亻	person	*rèn zì páng*
女	woman	*nǚ zì páng*
艹	grass	*cǎo zì tóu*
口	mouth	*kǒu zì páng*
灬; 火	fire	*huǒ zì páng*
讠	speech	*yán zì páng*

In mainland China, about 2,000 characters have been simplified, that is to say, some strokes have been either omitted or replaced with simpler strokes. The traditional form, or 'complex characters', is used in Hong Kong, Taiwan and other overseas Chinese communities. In this book, whenever there are two versions of the same character, the simplified form is used.

Calligraphy has always been regarded as a form of art in Chinese culture. Learning characters is a long process, so do not get frustrated if you find it difficult. Throughout the phrase book, both characters and pinyin are given.

the basics

*essentials

Hello.	你好。	*nǐ hǎo*
Goodbye.	再见。	*zàijiàn*
Good morning.	早上好。	*zǎoshàng hǎo*
Good evening.	晚上好。	*wǎnshàng hǎo*
Good night.	晚安。	*wǎn'ān*
Yes.	是的。	*shìde*
No.	不是。	*búshì*
Please (e.g. sit down).	请(坐)。	*qǐng (zuò)*
Thank you.	谢谢。	*xièxie*
You're welcome./ Don't mention it.	不客气/不谢。	*bú kèqì/ bú xiè*
I don't know.	我不知道。	*wǒ bù zhīdào*
I don't understand.	我不懂。	*wǒ bù dǒng*
I'm ill. I need to see a doctor.	我病了，需要看医生。	*wǒ bìng le, xūyào kàn yīshēng*
Please will you help me.	请帮我一下。	*qǐng bāng wǒ yīxià*
I need a taxi to the airport.	我需要一辆出租车去机场。	*wǒ xūyào yī liàng chūzūchē qù jīchǎng*
I've lost the key to my room.	我丢了我房间的钥匙。	*wǒ diū le wǒ fángjiān de yàoshi*
I only speak a little bit of Chinese.	我只说一点儿中文。	*wǒ zhǐ shuō yīdiǎnr Zhōngwén*
Is there anyone who speaks English?	这儿有人会说英文吗？	*zhèr yǒu rén huì shuō yīngwén ma*
Pardon?	什么？	*shénme*
Could you repeat that please?	你能再说一遍吗？	*nǐ néng zài shuō yī biàn ma*

More slowly, please.	请再慢一点儿。	*qǐng zài màn yīdiǎnr*
How do you say it in Chinese?	中文怎么说这个?	*Zhōngwén zěnme shuō zhège*
Excuse me./Sorry.	劳驾/对不起。	*láojià/ duìbùqǐ*
I'm sorry.	对不起。	*duìbùqǐ*
OK, fine./That's all right.	没关系。	*méi guānxì*
Cheers!	干杯!	*gān bēi*
I'd like...	我想要...	*wǒ xiǎng yào...*
Is/Are there (any)...?	有没有...?	*yǒu méi yǒu...*
Do you have...?	你有... 吗?	*nǐyǒu... ma*
What's this?	这是什么?	*zhè shì shénme*
How much is it?	多少钱?	*duō shǎo qián*
What time...?	几点...?	*jǐ diǎn...*
Can I...?	我可以...吗?	*wǒ kěyǐ... ma*
Can we...?	我们可以...吗?	*wǒmen kěyǐ... ma*
Where is/are...?	...在哪儿?	*... zài nǎr*
...the toilet/s	厕所...	*cèsuǒ...*
How do I/we get to...?	去...怎么走?	*qù... zěnme zǒu*
Can you...	你能不能...	*nǐ néng bù néng...*
tell me...?	告诉我...?	*gàosù wǒ...*
give me...?	给我...?	*gěi wǒ...*
show me on the map?	在地图上指给我看?	*zài dìtú shàng zhǐ gěi wǒ kàn*
write it down?	写下来?	*xiě xiàlái*
Help!	救命!	*jiùmìng*

✱ numbers

0	零	*líng*
1	一	*yī*
2	二	*èr*
3	三	*sān*
4	四	*sì*
5	五	*wǔ*
6	六	*liù*
7	七	*qī*
8	八	*bā*
9	九	*jiǔ*
10	十	*shí*
11	十一	*shíyī*
12...	十二...	*shí'èr...*
20	二十	*èrshí*
21	二十一	*èrshí'yī*
22...	二十二...	*èrshí'èr...*
30	三十	*sānshí*
31	三十一	*sānshí-yī*
32...	三十二...	*sānshí'èr...*
40	四十	*sìshí*
50	五十	*wǔshí*
99	九十九	*jiǔshí-jiǔ*
100	一百	*yī bǎi*
101	一百零一	*yī bǎi líng yī*
102...	一百零二...	*yī bǎi líng'èr...*
110	一百一十	*yī bǎi yīshí*
111	一百一十一	*yī bǎi yīshíyī*
112	一百一十二	*yī bǎi yīshí'èr*
113...	一百一十三...	*yī bǎi yīshísān...*
120	一百二十	*yī bǎi èrshí*
121...	一百二十一...	*yī bǎi èrshí-yī...*

200	二百	*èr bǎi*
250	二百五	*èr bǎi wǔ*
300...	三百...	*sān bǎi...*
1,000	一千	*yī qiān*
2,000	二千	*èr qiān*
3,000...	三千...	*sān qiān...*
10,000	一万	*yī wàn*
100,000	十万	*shí wàn*
one million	一百万	*yī bǎi wàn*
one and a half million	一百五十万	*yī bǎi wǔshí wàn*

There are two sets of Chinese script for numbers, each with the same pronunciation. For example, 'one' is represented by both 一 (yī) and 壹 (yī). One set is for normal use, and the other set with more complex characters is for banknotes and receipts.

	NORMAL USE	BANKNOTES AND RECEIPTS	
0	零	零	*líng*
1	一	壹	*yī*
2	二	贰	*èr*
3	三	三	*sān*
4	四	肆	*sì*
5	五	伍	*wǔ*
6	六	陆	*liù*
7	七	柒	*qī*
8	八	捌	*bā*
9	九	玖	*jiǔ*
10	十	拾	*shí*

ordinal numbers, fractions, days

二 (èr) and 两 (liǎng) both mean 'two'. 二 (èr) is used in counting and saying other numbers such as 'twenty-two' while 两 (liǎng) is used for telling the time and normally used to quantify things such as 'two books', 'two days', 'two hours', etc. (See **basic grammar**, page 167, for how to use numbers with nouns).

* ordinal numbers

first	第一	*dì yī*
second	第二	*dì'èr*
third	第三	*dì sān*
fourth	第四	*dì sì*
fifth	第五	*dì wǔ*
sixth	第六	*dì liù*
seventh	第七	*dì qī*
eighth	第八	*dì bā*
ninth	第九	*dì jiǔ*
tenth	第十	*dì shí*

* fractions

a quarter	四分之一	*sì fēn zhī yī*
a half	一半	*yī bàn*
three-quarters	四分之三	*sì fēn zhī sān*
a third	三分之一	*sān fēn zhī yī*
two-thirds	三分之二	*sān fēn zhī'èr*

* days

Monday	星期一	*xīngqīyī*
Tuesday	星期二	*xīngqī'èr*

Wednesday	星期三	*xīngqīsān*
Thursday	星期四	*xīngqīsì*
Friday	星期五	*xīngqīwǔ*
Saturday	星期六	*xīngqīliù*
Sunday	星期日/星期天	*xīngqīrì/ xīngqītiān*

* months

January	一月	*yīyuè*
February	二月	*èryuè*
March	三月	*sānyuè*
April	四月	*sìyuè*
May	五月	*wǔyuè*
June	六月	*liùyuè*
July	七月	*qīyuè*
August	八月	*bāyuè*
September	九月	*jiǔyuè*
October	十月	*shíyuè*
November	十一月	*shíyīyuè*
December	十二月	*shí'èryuè*

* years

1960	一九六零年	*yī jiǔ liù líng nián*
1978	一九七八年	*yī jiǔ qī bā nián*
2000	二零零零年	*èr líng líng líng nián*
2007	二零零七年	*èr líng líng qī nián*

年 (nián) means 'year' and must be used.

* seasons

spring	春天	*chūntiān*
summer	夏天	*xiàtiān*
autumn	秋天	*qiūtiān*
winter	冬天	*dōngtiān*

* dates

YOU MAY WANT TO SAY...

What day is it today?	今天是星期几?	*jīntiān shì xīngqī jǐ*
What date is it today?	今天是几号?	*jīntiān shì jǐ hào*
When is...	什么时候是...	*shénme shíhòu shì...*
your birthday?	你的生日?	*nǐde shēngrì*
Chinese New Year?	春节?	*chūn jié*
(It's) ...	(是)...	*(shì)...*
the fifteenth of April.	四月十五号。	*sìyuè shíwǔ hào*

* telling the time

YOU MAY WANT TO SAY...

What time is it?	几点了?	*jǐ diǎn le*
What time does it open?/close?	几点... 开门?/关门?	*jǐ diǎn... kāimén/ guānmén*
start?/finish?	开始?/结束?	*kāishǐ/ jiéshù*
It's...	现在(是)...	*xiànzài (shì)...*
10 o'clock	十点	*shí diǎn*
midday	中午	*zhōngwǔ*
At...	...	...
half past two	两点半	*liǎng diǎn bàn*
quarter past nine	九点一刻	*jiǔ diǎn yī kè*
quarter to ten	十点差一刻	*shí diǎn chā yī kè*
twenty past ten	十点二十	*shí diǎn èrshí*
precisely ten o'clock	十点整	*shí diǎn zhěng*
In...	...后	*... hòu*
ten minutes	十分钟	*shí fēnzhōng*
fifteen minutes	十五分钟	*shíwǔ fēnzhōng*
half an hour	半个小时	*bàn ge xiǎoshí*
an hour	一个小时	*yī ge xiǎoshí*

✱ time phrases

YOU MAY WANT TO SAY...

day	天	*tiān*
week	星期	*xīngqī*
weekend	周末	*zhōumò*
fortnight	每两个星期	*měi liǎng ge xīngqī*
month	月	*yuè*
year	年	*nián*
today	今天	*jīntiān*
tomorrow	明天	*míngtiān*
the day after tomorrow	后天	*hòu tiān*
yesterday	昨天	*zuótiān*
the day before yesterday	前天	*qián tiān*
this morning	今天早上	*jīntiān zǎoshàng*
this afternoon	今天下午	*jīntiān xiàwǔ*
this evening	今天晚上	*jīntiān wǎnshàng*
tonight	今晚	*jīnwǎn*
on Friday	星期五	*xīngqīwǔ*
every...	每个...	*měige...*
Friday	星期五	*xīngqīwǔ*
week	星期	*xīngqī*
for...	...	...
a week	一个星期	*yī ge xīngqī*
a month	一个月	*yī ge yuè*
I'm here for two weeks.	我在这儿呆两个星期。	*wǒ zài zhèr dāi liǎng ge xīngqī.*
I've been here for a month.	我来这儿已经一个月了。	*wǒ lái zhèr yǐjīng yī ge yuè le*

I've been learning Chinese for two years.	我已经学了两年中文了。	*wǒ yǐjīng xué le liǎng nián zhōngwén le*
next...	下个...	*xiàge...*
Tuesday	星期二	*xīngqī'èr*
next year	明年	*míng nián*
last...	上个...	*shàngge...*
week	星期	*xīngqī*
last night	昨晚	*zuó wǎn*
last year	去年	*qù nián*
...ago	...前	*... qián*
a week	一个星期	*yī ge xīngqī*
two years	两年	*liǎng nián*
Since...	自从...以来	*zìcóng... yǐlái*
yesterday	昨天	*zuótiān*
last month	上个月	*shàngge yuè*
(in) the morning/ afternoon	早上/下午	*zǎoshàng/ xiàwǔ*
in six months' time	六个月以后	*liù ge yuè yǐhòu*
(at) night	晚上	*wǎnshàng*
It's...	...	*...*
early	还早	*hái zǎo*
late	不早了	*bù zǎo le*

✱ measurements

MEASUREMENTS

centimetres	厘米	*límǐ*
metres	米	*mǐ*
kilometres	公里	*gōnglǐ*
li	里	*lǐ*
a litre	升	*shēng*
25 litres	25升	*25 shēng*
gramme	克	*kè*
100 grammes	一百克	*yī bǎi kè*
200 grammes	二百克	*èr bǎi kè*
kilo(s)	公斤	*gōngjīn*
jin	斤	*jīn*

CONVERSIONS

1km = *0.62 miles = 2 Chinese li*
1mile = *1.61km*
1litre = *1.8 pints*
100g = *3.5oz*
1oz = *28g*
1lb = *450g*
200g = *7oz*
¼1b = *113g*
¼kilo = *1.1lb*
½1b = *2.2lb*
1 kilo = *2.2lb*
1 kilo = *2 Chinese jin*

To convert kilometres to miles, divide by 8 and multiply by 5 e.g. 16 kilometres (16/8 = 2, 2x5 = 10) = 10 miles

For miles to kilometres: divide by 5 and multiply by 8 e.g. 50 miles (50/5 = 10, 10x8 = 80) = 80 kilometres

* clothes and shoe sizes

women's clothes

UK	6-8	8-10	12-14	16	18
China (cm)					
height	160-165	165-170	167-172	168-173	170-176
waist	84-86	88-90	92-96	98-102	106-110

men's clothes

UK	36	38-40	42	44	46
China (cm)					
height	165	170	175	180	185
waist	88-90	96-98	96-98	118-122	126-130

men's shirts

UK	14	14½	15-15½	16-16½	17
China (cm)	36-37	38-39	40-42	43-44	45-47

women's shoes

UK	4	4.5	5	5.5	6	6.5	7	7.5
China	35	36	37	38	39	40	42	40

men's shoes

UK	6	6.5	7	7.5	8	8.5	9	9.5
China	39	40	41	42	43	44	45	46

* national holidays

- Shops, theatres, cinemas and museums remain open on all public holidays and festivals. Business and government offices usually close for a week during May Holiday and Chinese New Year. The dates given below are the Western dates.

元旦	*yuán dàn*	New Year's Day: 1 January
春节	*chūnjié*	Chinese New Year
正月初一	*zhèngyuè chūyī*	Chinese New Year's Day: Late January or early February
元宵节	*yuánxiāo jié*	Lantern Festival: Early February or late February
劳动节	*láodòng jié*	May Labour Day: 1 May
国庆节	*guóqìing jié*	National Day: 1 October
中秋节	*zhōngqiú jié*	Moon Festival/Mid Autumn Festival: Early September

* Chinese animal signs

● In the Chinese lunar calendar, each year is associated with an animal sign. There are 12 signs which come round every 12 years. The dragon is regarded as a lucky sign.

2007	Pig	猪	*zhū*
2008	Rat	鼠	*shǔ*
2009	Ox	牛	*niú*
2010	Tiger	虎	*hǔ*
2011	Rabbit	兔	*tù*
2012	Dragon	龙	*lóng*
2013	Snake	蛇（小 龙）	*shé (xiǎo lóng)*
2014	Horse	马	*mǎ*
2015	Sheep	羊	*yáng*
2016	Monkey	猴	*hóu*
2017	Rooster	鸡	*jī*
2018	Dog	狗	*gǒu*

general conversation

greetings

The most common greeting Nǐ hǎo (lit. you good/well), a general expression for 'hello', is used throughout the day. Zǎoshàng hǎo (lit. morning good) or simply zǎo is used but not as extensively as 'Good morning' is in English. The Chinese equivalents of 'Good afternoon' and 'Good evening' are rarely used.

✱ greetings

YOU MAY WANT TO SAY...

Hello.	你好。	*nǐ hǎo*
Good morning.	早上好；早。	*zǎoshàng hǎo; zǎo*
Good night.	晚安。	*wǎn'ān*
Goodbye./Bye.	再见。	*zàijiàn*
See you later.	回见。	*huí jiàn*
How are you?		
(formal)	您好吗？	*nín hǎo ma?*
(informal)	怎么样？	*zěnme yàng*
How are things?	还好吗？	*hái hǎo ma*
Fine, thanks.	好，谢谢。	*hǎo, xièxie*
And you?		
(formal)	您呢？	*nín ne*
(informal)	你呢？	*nǐ ne*

✱ introductions

In Chinese, family names/surnames are placed before given names. Titles, when used, are placed either after family names or at the end of the full name. The most common way of addressing a Chinese person is to use his/her full name. Chinese women do not change their family names after they get married.

YOU MAY WANT TO SAY...

My name is...	我叫...	*wǒ jiào...*
My family name is...	我姓...	*wǒ xìng...*
This is...	这是...	*zhè shì...*
Mr Brown	布朗先生	*bùlwǎng xiānshēng*
my husband	我的丈夫	*wǒde zhàngfū*
my son	我的儿子	*wǒde érzi*
my boyfriend	我的男朋友	*wǒde nán péngyou*
my fiancé	我的未婚夫	*wǒde wèihūnfū*
This is...	这是...	*zhè shì...*
Miss Brown	布朗小姐	*bùlǎng xiǎojiě*
Mrs Brown	布朗太太	*bùlǎng tàitai*
my wife	我的太太	*wǒde tàitai*
my daughter	我的女儿	*wǒde nǚ'ér*
my girlfriend	我的女朋友	*wǒde nǚ péngyou*
my fiancée	我的未婚妻	*wǒde wèihūnqī*
Pleased to meet you (singular).	很高兴见到你。	*hěn gāoxìng jiàndào nǐ*
Pleased to meet you (plural).	很高兴见到你们。	*hěn gāoxìng jiàndào nǐmen*

* talking about yourself

- Kinship terms are rather complex in Chinese. For example, 兄弟姐妹 (*xiōng dì jiě mèi*) is a general term for 'brothers and sisters', and there are four specific terms: 哥哥 (*gēge*) 'elder brother', 弟弟 (*dìdi*) 'younger brother', 姐姐 (*jiějie*) 'elder sister' and 妹妹 (*mèimei*) 'younger sister'.

YOU MAY WANT TO SAY...

• I'm English.	我是英国人。	*wǒ shì yīngguórén*
• I'm Irish.	我是爱尔兰人。	*wǒ shì ài'ěrlánrén*
• I'm Scottish.	我是威尔士人。	*wǒ shì sūgélánrén*
• I'm Welsh.	我是苏格兰人。	*wǒ shì wēi'ěrshìrén*
• I come from...	我从...来	*wǒ cóng...lái*
England	英格兰	*yīnggélán*
Ireland	爱尔兰	*ài'ěrlán*
Scotland	苏格兰	*sūgélán*
Wales	威尔士	*wēi'ěrshì*
• I/We live in...	我/我们住在...	*wǒ/wǒmen zhù zài...*
London	伦敦	*lúndūn*
• I'm 25 years old.	我二十五岁。	*wǒ èrshí wǔ suì*
• He's/she's five years old.	他/她五岁。	*tā/tā wǔ suì*
• I'm a...	我是...	*wǒ shì...*
web designer	网络设计师	*wǎngluò shèjìshī*
student	学生	*xuéshēng*
• I work in/for...	我为...工作	*wǒ wéi... gōngzuò*
a bank	一家银行	*yī jiā yínháng*
• I'm unemployed.	我没有工作。	*wǒ méi yǒu gōngzuò*
• I'm self-employed.	我是个体户。	*wǒ shì gètǐhù*

I'm a freelancer.	我是自由职业者。	*wǒ shì zìyóu zhíyèzhě*
I'm...	我...	*wǒ...*
married	结婚了	*jiéhūn le*
divorced	离婚了	*líhūn le*
separated	分居了	*fēnjū le*
single	单身	*dānshēn*
I'm a...	我的...去世了	*wǒde... qùshì le*
widower	妻子	*qīzi*
widow	丈夫	*zhàngfū*
I have ...	我有...	*wǒ yǒu...*
three children	三个孩子	*sān ge háizi*
four brothers	四个兄弟	*sì ge xiōngdì*
two sisters	两个姐妹	*liǎng ge jiěmèi*
I don't have...	我没有...	*wǒ méi yǒu...*
any children	孩子	*háizi*
any brothers or sisters	兄弟姐妹	*xiōngdì jiěmèi*
I'm on holiday here.	我来这儿度假。	*wǒ lái zhèr dùjià*
I'm here on business.	我来这儿出差。	*wǒ lái zhèr chūchāi*
I'm here with my...	我的... 也在这儿	*wǒde... yě zài zhèr*
family	家人	*jiārén*
colleague	同事	*tóngshì*
My son/daughter is...	我的儿子/女儿是...	*wǒde érzi/nǚ'ér shì...*
My husband/wife works in...	我的丈夫/妻子在...工作。	*wǒde zhàngfū/qīzi zài... gōngzuò*
I speak very little Chinese.	我说一点点中文。	*wǒ shuō yīdiǎndiǎn zhōngwén*

* asking about other people

YOU MAY WANT TO SAY...

• Where do you come from?	你从哪儿来?	*nǐ cóng nǎr lái*
• What's your name?	你叫什么?	*nǐ jiào shénme*
• Are you married?	你结婚了吗?	*nǐ jiéhūn le ma*
• Do you have...	你有	*nǐ yǒu...*
any children?	孩子/小孩吗?	*háizi/xiǎohái ma*
any brothers and sisters?	兄弟姐妹吗?	*xiōngdì jiěmèi ma*
a girlfriend?	女朋友吗?	*nǚ péngyou ma*
a boyfriend?	男朋友吗?	*nán péngyou ma*
• How old are you/they?	你/他们多大了?	*nǐ/tāmen duō dà le*
• Is this your...	这是你的...吗?	*zhè shì nǐde... ma*
husband/wife?	丈夫/妻子	*zhàngfū/qīzi*
friend?	朋友	*péngyǒu*
• Where are you going?	你去哪儿?	*nǐ qù nǎr*
• Which hotel are you staying at?	你住在哪家饭店?	*nǐ zhù zài nǎ jiā fàndiàn*
• Where do you live?	你住在哪儿?	*nǐ zhù zài nǎr*
• What do you do?	你干什么工作?	*nǐ gàn shénme gōngzuò*

* chatting

YOU MAY WANT TO SAY...

Beijing is very beautiful.	北京真漂亮。	*běijīng zhēn piāoliàng*
I like the Great Wall very much.	我特别喜欢长城。	*wǒ tèbié xǐhuān cháng chéng*
It's the first time I've been to China.	这是我第一次来中国。	*zhè shì wǒ dì yī cì lái zhōngguó*
I come to Shanghai often.	我常常来上海。	*wǒ chángcháng lái shànghǎi*
Are you from here?	你是本地人吗?	*nǐ shì běndìrén ma?*
Have you ever been to...	你去过...吗?	*nǐ qù guò... ma?*
Edinburgh?	爱丁堡	*àidīngbǎo*
Hong Kong?	香港	*xiāng gǎng*
Did you like it?	你喜欢那儿吗?	*nǐ xǐhuān nàr ma*

YOU MAY HEAR...

我是你的/你们的翻译。	*wǒ shì nǐde/ nǐmende fānyì*	I'm your interpreter.
请叫我...	*qǐng jiào wǒ...*	Please call me...
这是我的爱人。	*zhè shì wǒde àirén*	This is my wife/ husband.
你喜欢中国吗?	*nǐ xǐhuān zhōngguó ma*	Do you like China?

你以前去过深圳吗？	*nǐ yǐqián qù guò shēnzhèn ma*	Have you been to Shenzhen before?
你在这儿呆多久？	*nǐ zài zhè'ér dāi duō jiǔ*	How long are you here for?
你的中文很好。	*nǐde zhōngwén hěn hǎo*	Your Chinese is very good.
你多大了？	*nǐ duō dà le*	How old are you?
你结婚了吗？	*nǐ jiéhūn le ma*	Are you married?

Don't be offended if a Chinese person asks about your age and marital status as these are perceived as friendly questions. The term áirén (lit. love person) is commonly used in mainland China to refer to a spouse. Other terms for 'wife' and 'husband' are: tàitai/jīzi (wife) and xiānsheng /zhàngfu (husband).

* the weather

YOU MAY WANT TO SAY...

What fantastic weather!	天气真好！	*tiānqì zhēn hǎo*
It's (very)...	天气(很)...	*tiānqì(hěn)...*
hot	热	*rè*
cold	冷	*lěng*
It's windy.	风很大。	*fēng hěn dà*

What's the forecast?	天气预报怎么说?	*tiānqì yùbào zěnme shuō*
It's...	正在...	*zhèngzài...*
raining	下雨	*xiàyǔ*
snowing	下雪	*xiàxuě*

* likes and dislikes

YOU MAY WANT TO SAY...

I like...	我喜欢...	*wǒ xǐhuān...*
strawberries	草莓	*cǎoméi*
I love the beach.	我爱海滩。	*wǒ ài hǎitān*
I don't like ...	我不喜欢...	*wǒ bù xǐhuān...*
the rain	下雨	*xiàyǔ*
I hate swimming.	我恨游泳。	*wǒ hèn yóuyǒng*
Do you like...	你喜欢...吗?	*nǐ xǐhuān... ma*
Chinese tea?	中国茶	*zhōngguó chá*
I like it/them.	我喜欢。	*wǒ xǐhuān*
I don't like it/them.	我不喜欢。	*wǒ bù xǐhuān*

* feelings and opinions

YOU MAY WANT TO SAY...

Are you...	你...吗?	*nǐ... ma*
all right?	都好	*dōu hǎo*
Are you (very)...	你(很)...吗?	*nǐ(hěn)...ma*
cold?	冷	*lěng*
hot?	热	*rè*

feelings and opinions

I'm (just)...	我(不过)...	*wǒ(bú guò)...*
tired	累了	*lèi le*
I'm a bit annoyed.	我有一些生气。	*wǒ yǒu yīxiē shēngqì*
What do you think of...?	你觉得...怎么样?	*nǐ juéde...zěnme yàng*
I/We think/thought it's...	我/我们觉得...	*wǒ/wǒmen juéde...*
great	棒极了	*bàngjíle*
pathetic	可悲	*kěbēi*
funny	真滑稽	*zhēn huájī*
awful	糟透了	*zāotòule*
Don't you like it?	你不喜欢吗?	*nǐ bù xǐhuān ma*
Do you like him/her?	你喜欢他/她吗?	*nǐ xǐhuān tā/tā ma*
I like him/her.	我喜欢他/她	*wǒ xǐhuān tā/tā*
What's your favourite...?	你最喜欢的...是什么?	*nǐ zuì xǐhuān de...shì shénme*
film	电影	*diànyǐng*
food	饭	*fàn*
My favourite... is...	我最喜欢的...是...	*wǒ zuì xǐhuān de...shì...*
How do people feel about...	人们对...有什么看法?	*rénmen duì...yǒu shénme kànfǎ*
the government?	政府	*zhèngfǔ*
the British?	英国人	*yīngguórén*
drugs?	毒品	*dúpǐn*

✱ making arrangements

YOU MAY WANT TO SAY...

What are you doing tonight?	你今晚做什么?	*nǐ jīnwǎn zuò shénmo*
Would you like...	你想...吗?	*nǐ xiǎng...ma*
a drink?	喝一杯	*hē yī bēi*
something to eat?	吃点儿什么	*chī diǎnr shénme*
to come with us?	和我们一起来	*hé wǒmen yīqǐ lái*
Yes, please.	想,谢谢。	*xiǎng, xièxie*
No, thank you.	不想,谢谢。	*bù xiǎng, xièxie*
I'd love to.	太想了。	*tài xiǎng le*
What time shall we meet?	我们几点碰头?	*wǒmen jǐ diǎn pèngtóu*
Where shall we meet?	我们在哪儿碰头?	*wǒmen zài nǎr pèngtóu*
See you...	...见。	*...jiàn*
later.	一会儿	*yīhuìr*
at seven.	七点	*qī diǎn*
We're looking forward to it.	我们盼着呢。	*wǒmen pàn zhe ne*
Sorry, we already have plans.	对不起,我们已经有安排了。	*duìbùqǐ, wǒmen yǐjīng yǒu ānpái le*
Please go away.	请走开。	*qǐng zǒu kāi*
Leave us alone!	别打扰我们!	*bié dǎrǎo wǒmen*
What's your email address?	你的电子邮址是什么?	*nǐde diànzǐ yóuzhǐ shì shénme*
My email address is...	我的电子邮址是...	*wǒde diànzǐ yóuzhǐ shì...*

* useful expressions

(see **essentials**, page 16)

YOU MAY WANT TO SAY...

Congratulations!	祝贺/恭喜!	*zhùhè/gōngxǐ*
Happy Birthday!	生日快乐!	*shēngrì kuàilè*
Happy Christmas!	圣诞快乐!	*shèngdàn kuàilè*
Happy New Year!	新年好!	*xīn nián hǎo*
Good luck!	好运气!	*hǎo yùnqì*
That's fantastic!	太棒了!	*tài bàng le*
That's terrible!	太糟了!	*tài zāo le*
What a pity!	太可惜了!	*tài kěxí le*
Have a good journey!	一路顺利!	*yī lù shùnlì*
Enjoy your meal!	慢用!	*màn yòng*
Thank you.	谢谢。	*xièxie*
Cheers (when toasting)!	干杯!	*gānbēi*

* business trips

- Titles are important in Chinese business circles. Job titles such as 'manager', 'director' are used as forms of address as well as forms of reference. For example, if someone's surname is Wáng and s/he is a manager, s/he will be referred to as Wáng jīnglǐ (*lit.* Wang manager). So, it is very important that you find out not only the names of the people you are going to meet, but also their job titles and positions in terms of seniority.

- When you meet your business partner(s) for the first time, always dress formally and exchange business cards after the hand-shaking. If you do not know how to say the person's title in Chinese, you can use their surname followed by xiāngsheng (Mr), xiǎojie (Miss) to address young women, or nǚshì (Madam) to address older women.

- A welcome banquet is usually held on the day of your arrival. The host always makes a welcome speech and expects the most senior person in the guest group to say something as well. It is very important that you bring some gifts from home with you so that you can give them to your business partners after the speech. Gift-giving is seen as a desire to start or maintain a good relationship. Clocks and knives are culturally inappropriate gifts as the phrase 'to give clocks' in Chinese sounds like 'to send someone to death' and giving someone a knife can be taken as a signal of ending a relationship.

useful words and expressions

YOU MAY SEE...

广告部	*guǎnggào bù*	advertising department
董事会	*dǒngshìhuì*	board
主席	*zhǔxí*	chairman
总工程师	*zǒng gōngchéngshī*	chief engineer
总裁	*zǒng cái*	chief executive
会议室	*huìyì shì*	conference room
副经理	*fù jīnglǐ*	deputy manager
主任	*zhǔrèn*	director
经理	*jīnglǐ*	manager
厂长	*chǎngcháng*	manager (of a factory)
总经理	*zǒng jīnglǐ*	managing director
部长	*bùzhǎng*	minister
人事部	*rénshì bù*	personnel department
销售部	*xiāoshòu bù*	sales department

* useful words and expressions

YOU MAY HEAR...

名片	*míng piàn*	business card
公司	*gōngsī*	company
总部	*zǒngbù*	headquarters
有限公司	*yǒuxiàn gōngsī*	limited company
谈判	*tánpàn*	negotiation
秘书	*mìshū*	secretary
失败	*shībài*	to fail, failure
签合同	*qiān hétóng*	to sign the contract
成功	*chénggōng*	to succeed, success

* first meeting

YOU MAY WANT TO SAY...

Very pleased to meet you.	很高兴见到您。	*hěn gāoxìng jiàndào nín*
How do you do!	您好！	*nín hǎo*
I work for...	我为...工作	*wǒ wéi... gōngzuò*
What should I call you?	我该怎么称呼您?	*wǒ gāi zěnme chēnghū nín*
I'd like to see...	我想见一下...	*wǒ xiǎng jiàn yīxià...*
I have an appointment with...	我和...有约会。	*wǒ hé... yǒu yuēhuì*
What time will he/she be back?	他/她几点能回来?	*tā/tā jǐ diǎn néng huílái*
Can I wait here for a while?	我在这儿等一会儿，行吗?	*wǒ zài zhèr děng yīhuìr, xíng ma*
Can I leave a message?	我可以留个口信吗?	*wǒ kěyǐ liú ge kǒuxìn ma*
Please give this note to him/her.	请把这张条子给他/她。	*qǐng bǎ zhè zhāng tiáozi gěi tā/tā*
Can you ask him to call me please?	能告诉他给我打个电话吗?	*néng gàosù tā gěi wǒ dǎ ge diànhuà ma*
This is my mobile/hotel number.	这是我的手机号/饭店电话号码。	*zhè shì wǒde shǒujī hào/fàndiàn diànhuà hàomǎ*

YOU MAY HEAR...

幸会。	*xìng huì*	Pleased to meet you.
您好！有事吗？	*nín hǎo yǒu shì ma*	Hello, can I help you?
您贵姓？	*nín guì xìng*	What's your surname?
您找谁？	*nín zhǎo shéi*	Whom are you looking for?
您是哪个公司的？	*nín shì nǎge gōngsīde*	Which company do you work for?
一路顺利吗？	*yīlù shùnlì ma*	Did you have a good journey?
欢迎您来我们公司	*huānyíng nín lái wǒmen gōngsī*	Welcome to our company.
这是我的名片。	*zhè shì wǒde míngpiàn*	This is my business card.
您可以给我一张您的名片吗？	*nín kěyǐ gěi wǒ yī zhāng nínde míngpiàn ma*	May I have your business card, please?

Note the use of the polite pronoun for 'you' '您' (*nín*) instead of 你 (*nǐ*).

* business meetings

YOU MAY WANT TO SAY...

Shall we have another meeting?	我们再见一次，好吗？	*wǒmen zài jiàn yīcì, hǎo ma*

Where is the interpreter?	翻译在哪儿?	*fānyì zài nǎr*
Could you explain it again?	您再解释一遍, 好吗?	*nín zài jiěshì yībiàn, hǎo ma*
Have I understood it correctly?	我这么理解, 对吗?	*wǒ zhème lǐjiě, duì ma*
What do you think?	您觉得怎么样?	*nín juéde zěnme yàng*
Please consider the matter.	请考虑这件事。	*qǐng kǎolǜ zhè jiàn shì*
Shall we talk it over again?	我们再谈谈, 好吗?	*wǒmen zài tántan, hǎo ma*
Is there anything you are not happy about?	有什么您不满意的地方吗?	*yǒu shénme nín bù mǎnyì de dìfāng ma*
Are you ready to sign the contract?	你们可以签合同了吗?	*nǐmen kěyǐ qiān hétóng le ma*
When are we going to sign the contract?	我们什么时候签合同?	*wǒmen shénme shíhòu qiān hétóng*
Thank you for your understanding and support.	谢谢你们的理解和支持。	*xièxie nǐmen de lǐjiě hé zhīchí*
I wish our collaboration every success.	祝我们合作成功。	*zhù wǒmen hézuò chénggōng*
I hope we'll meet again.	希望我们还会见面。	*xīwàng wǒmen hái huì jiànmiàn*
See you in London.	伦敦见。	*lúndūn jiàn*

YOU MAY HEAR...

好主意。	*hǎo zhǔyì*	Good idea.
看情况。	*kàn qíngkuàng*	It depends.
我考虑一下	*wǒ kǎolǜ yīxià*	I'll think about it.
要请示一下	*yào qǐngshì yīxià*	It needs permission from the top.
不可能。	*bù kěnéng*	Impossible.
我不同意。	*wǒ bù tóngyì*	I disagree.
让您久等了。	*ràng nín jiǔ děng le*	Sorry to have kept you waiting.
他/她不在。	*tā/tā bú zài*	He/She is not in.
他/她正在开会。	*tā/tā zhèngzài kāihuì*	He/She is at a meeting.
您愿意等一会儿吗?	*nín yuànyì děng yīhuìr ma*	Would you like to wait?

* living in China

YOU MAY WANT TO SAY...

I'm here...	我来这儿...	*wǒ lái zhèr...*
teaching English	教英文	*jiào yīngwén*
for a conference	开会	*kāihuì*
on a lecturing tour	讲学	*jiǎngxué*
studying Chinese	学中文	*xué zhōngwén*

Our company has an office in Beijing.	我们公司在北京有个办事处。	*wǒmen gōngsī zài běijīng yǒuge bànshìchǔ*
I have been here for...	我来这儿已经...了	*wǒ lái zhèr yǐjīng...le*
four weeks	四个星期	*sì ge xīngqī*
I'm staying for a year in total.	我一共呆一年。	*wǒ yīgòng dāi yī nián*

✱ social occasions

YOU MAY WANT TO SAY...

Please accept our gift.	请收下我们的礼物。	*qǐng shōuxià wǒmen de lǐwù*
You're too generous.	你太客气了	*nǐ tài kèqì le*
This is beautiful.	真漂亮！	*zhēn piāoliàng*
Let's drink to a successful collaboration.	祝合作成功。	*zhù hézuò chénggōng*
I don't drink.	我不喝酒	*wǒ bù hē jiǔ*
To your good health.	祝你身体健康！	*zhù nǐ shēntǐ jiànkāng*
Thank you for everything.	谢谢你为我们做的一切。	*xièxie nǐ wéi wǒmen zuò de yīqiē*
The dinner was superb.	这顿晚餐非常好。	*zhè dùn wǎncān fēicháng hǎo*

YOU MAY HEAR...

哪里，哪里。	*nǎli, nǎli*	**Not at all** (as a response to a compliment).
过奖。	*guòjiǎng*	**I'm flattered** (as a response to a compliment).
这是我们的一点儿心意。	*zhè shì wǒmen de yīdiǎnr xīnyì*	**This is a very small present.**
请笑纳。	*qǐng xiào nà*	**Please accept such a small gift.**
谢谢你的礼物。	*xièxie nǐde lǐwù*	**Thank you for your present.**
我会珍惜它的。	*wǒ huì zhēnxí tā de*	**I will treasure it.**
我想请你出去吃饭。	*wǒ xiǎng qǐng nǐ chūqu chīfàn*	**I'd like to take you out for a meal.**
我请客。	*wǒ qǐngkè*	**It's my treat.**

travel&transport

* arriving in the country

YOU MAY SEE...

行李提取/行李认领	*xínglǐ tíqǔ/ xínglǐ rènlǐng*	baggage reclaim
海关	*hǎiguān*	customs
出口	*chūkǒu*	exit
入境检查	*rùjìng jiǎnchá*	immigration
中国边防检查	*zhōngguó biānfáng jiǎnchá*	passport control
转乘国内航班	*zhuǎnchéng guónèi hángbān*	transfer to domestic flights

YOU MAY WANT TO SAY...

I am here...	我来...	*wǒ lái...*
on holiday	度假	*dù jiǎ*
on business	出差	*chū chāi*
It's for my own personal use.	这是我自己用的。	*zhè shì wǒ zìjǐ yòng de*

YOU MAY HEAR...

请出示你的护照。	*qǐng chūshì nǐde hùzhào*	Your passport please.
你将停留多久?	*nǐ jiāng tíngliú duō jiǔ*	How long are you going to stay here?
你要去什么地方?	*nǐ yào qù shénme dìfāng*	Where are you going?

你此行的目的是什么？	*nǐ cǐ xíng de mùdì shì shénme*	What is the purpose of your visit?
请打开…	*qǐng dǎkāi…*	Please open…
这个包/箱子	*zhè ge bāo/ xiāngzi*	this bag/ suitcase.
请跟我来	*qǐng gēn wǒ lái*	Come along with me please.

* directions

YOU MAY SEE...

机场	*jīchǎng*	airport
机场巴士	*jīchǎng bāshì*	airport bus
公共汽车总站	*gōnggòng qìchē zǒngzhàn*	bus station
闲人免进	*xián rén miǎn jìn*	no trespassing
行人	*xíngrén*	pedestrians
私人住宅	*sīrén zhùzhái*	private property
火车站	*huǒchē zhàn*	railway station
出租车，的士	*chūzūchē, díshì*	taxi
通向…	*tōng xiàng…*	to the…
地铁	*dìtiě*	underground
东	*dōng*	east
南	*nán*	south
西	*xī*	west
北	*běi*	north
左	*zuǒ*	left
右	*yòu*	right

directions

YOU MAY WANT TO SAY...

Excuse me, please.	对不起	*duìbùqǐ*
Where is...	...在哪儿?	*... zài nǎr*
the cash point?	现钞机	*xiànchāo jī*
the toilet?	厕所	*cèsuǒ*
How do we get to...	去...怎么走?	*qù... zěnme zǒu*
the airport?	机场	*jīchǎng*
I'm lost.	我迷路了	*wǒ mílù le*
Is this the right way to... ?	这是去...的路吗?	*zhè shì qù... de lù ma*
Can you show me on the map, please?	你能在地图上指给我看吗?	*nǐ néng zài dìtú shàng zhǐ gěi wǒ kàn ma*
Is it far?	远吗?	*yuǎn ma*
Is there... near here?	附近有...吗?	*fùjìn yǒu... ma*
an internet café	网吧	*wǎng bā*
Where is the nearest...?	最近的...在哪儿?	*zuìjìn de... zài nǎr*

YOU MAY HEAR...

我们现在在这个位置	*wǒmen xiànzài zài zhè ge wèizhì*	We are here.
这边走	*zhèbiān zǒu*	This way.
直走	*zhí zǒu*	Straight on.
往... 拐 右	*wǎng... guǎi* *yòu*	Turn... right

travel and transport

走... 第一个路口	*zǒu... dì yī ge lùkǒu*	Take the first on the...
左边的	*zuǒbiān de*	left.
在...	*zài...*	It's...
对面	*duìmiàn*	opposite
后面	*hòumiàn*	behind
附近	*fùjìn*	next to
很近/很远	*hěn jìn/hěn yuǎn*	It's very near/far away.
离这儿五分钟	*lí zhèr wǔ fēnzhōng*	It's five minutes away.
你得坐...路公共汽车	*nǐ děi zuò...lù gōnggòng qìchē*	You have to take bus number...

* information and tickets

(see **telling the time**, page 23)

- The easiest way to buy tickets is to go through a travel agent or a ticket agent. Alternatively, you can book them through your hotel.

YOU MAY WANT TO SAY...

Is there a train/ bus/boat to... today?	今天有去...的火车/汽车/船吗?	*jīntiān yǒu qù... de huǒchē/qìchē/ chuán ma*
What time is the... to Xi'an?	去西安的... 是几点?	*qù xī'ān de... shì jǐ diǎn*
next train	下一趟火车	*xià yī tàng huǒchē*
first bus	首车	*shǒu chē*

information and tickets

What time does it arrive in...?	几点到...?	*jǐ diǎn dào...*
Do I have to change?	我需要换车吗?	*wǒ xūyào huàn chē ma*
Which platform for...?	去...是几站台?	*qù...shì jǐ zhàntái*
Which bus stop for...?	去...是哪个公共汽车站?	*qù...shì nǎge gōnggòng qìchē zhàn*
Where can I buy...	我能在哪儿买到...?	*wǒ néng zài nǎr mǎi dào...*
a ticket?	票	*piào*
One/two... tickets to Shanghai please.	请给我一张/两张去上海的...票	*qǐng gěi wǒ yī zhāng/liǎng zhāng qù shànghǎi de... piào*
Single	单程	*dānchéng*
Return	往返	*wǎngfǎn*
For...	(...)	*(...)*
two adults	两个成人	*liǎng ge chéngrén*
two children	两个小孩	*liǎng ge xiǎohái*
Is there a fee?	有手续费吗?	*yǒu shǒuxù fèi ma*
Is there a discount for...	...享有折扣吗?	*xiǎngyǒu zhékòu ma*
students?	学生	*xuéshēng*
senior citizens?	老年人	*lǎonián rén*

YOU MAY HEAR...

...点离开, 出发, 开	*...diǎn lí kāi, chūfā, kāi*	It leaves at...
...点到达, 到站, 到	*...diǎn dàodá, dàozhàn, dào*	It arrives at...
每十分钟一趟。	*měi shí fēnzhōng yī tàng*	They go every ten minutes.
你得换。	*nǐ děi huàn*	You have to change.
四号站台/码头。	*sì hào zhàntái/ mǎtóu*	It's platform/pier number four.
你想什么时候...?	*nǐ xiǎng shénme shíhòu ...*	When do you want to...
旅行	*lǚxíng*	travel?
回来	*huílái*	come back?
单程还是往返?	*dānchéng háishì wǎngfǎn*	Single or return?
吸烟区还是不吸烟区?	*xīyān qū háishì bù xīyān qū*	Smoking or non-smoking?
要额外加...	*yào éwài jiā...*	There's a supplement of...

* air travel

(see **information and tickets**, page 53)

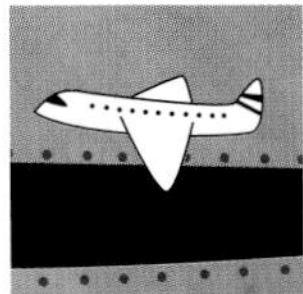

For international departures, you must complete a departure card. In Beijing there are several bus services from the airport. To make sure you are on the right bus, show the driver the address in Chinese.

YOU MAY SEE...

到达/到港	*dàodá/dàogǎng*	**arrivals**
中国银行	*zhōngguó yínháng*	**Bank of China**
登机	*dēngjī*	**boarding**
租车	*zū chē*	**car hire**
候机厅	*hòujī tīng*	**departure lounge**
国内出发	*guónèi chūfā*	**domestic departures**
紧急出口	*jǐnjí chūkǒu*	**emergency exit**
国际出发	*guójì chūfā*	**international departures**
中国边防检查	*zhōngguó biānfáng jiǎnchá*	**passport control**
洗手间	*xǐshǒujiān*	**toilets**

YOU MAY WANT TO SAY...

I want to change/ cancel my ticket.	我想换票/退票	*wǒ xiǎng huàn piào/ tuì piào*

I need...	我要…	*wǒ yào...*
an aisle seat	一个靠走廊的座位	*yīge kào zǒuláng de zuòwèi*
a window seat	一个靠窗户的座位	*yīge kào chuānghù de zuòwèi*
Is there a delay?	晚点了吗?	*wǎndiǎn le ma*
Which gate is it?	这是几号登机口?	*zhè shì jǐ hào dēng jī kǒu*
My luggage hasn't arrived.	我的行李还没有到。	*wǒde xínglǐ hái méi yǒu dào*
Is there a bus/ train to the centre of town?	有进城的班车/火车吗?	*yǒu jìn chéng de bānchē/ huǒchē ma*

WORDS TO LISTEN OUT FOR...

取消	*qǔxiāo*	cancelled
延误/晚点	*yánwù/wǎndiǎn*	delay
航班	*hángbān*	flight
登机口	*dēngjī kǒu*	gate
最后呼叫	*zuìhòu hūjiào*	last call

* taxis

(see **directions**, page 51)

YOU MAY SEE...

出租车/的士	*chūzūchē/díshì*	taxi
空车	*kōngchē*	unoccupied

taxis

YOU MAY WANT TO SAY...

Is there a taxi rank round here?	这儿有出租车站吗?	*zhèr yǒu chūzūchē zhàn ma*
Can you call me a taxi immediately?	你能马上替我叫一辆出租吗?	*nǐ néng mǎshàng tì wǒ jiào yī liàng chūzū ma*
Can you order me a taxi for tomorrow at 9am?	你能替我订一辆出租车吗? 明天早上九点走。	*nǐ néng tì wǒ dìng yī liàng chūzūchē ma? míngtiān zǎoshàng jiǔ diǎn zǒu.*
To this address, please.	请带我去这个地址。	*qǐng dài wǒ qù zhège dìzhǐ*
How much will it cost?	多少钱?	*duō shǎo qián*
I'm in a hurry.	我有急事。	*wǒ yǒu jíshì*
Stop here, please.	请在这儿停	*qǐng zài zhèr tíng*
Can you wait for me, please?	请你等我一下, 好吗?	*qǐng nǐ děng wǒ yīxià, hǎo ma*
I think there's a mistake.	我觉得有问题	*wǒ juéde yǒu wèntí*
On the meter it's 20 yuan.	表上说20元。	*biǎo shàng shuō èrshí yuán*
Keep the change.	不用找了。	*bù yòng zhǎo le*
Can you give me a receipt for 30 yuan?	你能给我一张30元的收据吗?	*nǐ néng gěi wǒ yī zhāng sāshí yuán de shōujù ma*

WORDS TO LISTEN OUT FOR...

大概三十五元。	*dàgài sānshíwǔ yuán*	**It'll cost about 35 yuan.**
一共十八元。	*yīgòng shíbā yuán*	**That's eighteen yuan.**
附加...等人时间。	*fùjiā... děng rén shíjiān*	**There's a supplement... for waiting time.**

* trains

(see **information and tickets**, page 53)

All passenger trains in China are numbered. In general, trains with one or two digits are fast trains while those with three digits are usually slow trains that have many stops. On long distance trains, you have three choices: soft-sleepers, hard-sleepers or hard-seats. Each soft-sleeper compartment contains four small berths (like two sets of bunk beds). Hard-sleeper berths are divided into upper, middle and lower. If you travel by hard-sleeper or hard-seat, you need to bring your own cup.

Between some big cities such as Beijing and Shanghai, there are express trains which only stop at major stations and the seats are like airline seats.

trains

YOU MAY SEE...

预定票	*yùdìng piào*	advance booking
到站	*dàozhàn*	arrivals
目的地	*mùdìdì*	destination
入口	*rùkǒu*	entrance
收费休息室	*shōufèi xiūxí shì*	fee-paying lounge
行李寄存	*xínglǐ jìcún*	left luggage
失物招领	*shīwù zhāolǐng*	lost property
行李锁柜	*xínglǐ suǒguì*	luggage lockers
母婴候车区	*mǔyīng hòuchē qū*	mother-baby waiting area
罚款	*fákuǎn*	penalty
站台	*zhàntái*	platform
预订	*yùdìng*	reservations
车票	*chēpiào*	tickets
候车室	*hòuchē shì*	waiting room

YOU MAY WANT TO SAY...

I'd like a single/ return ticket to... please.	*wǒ xiǎng yào yī zhāng qù... de dānchéng/wǎngfǎn piào*	我想要一张/去...的单程/往返票。
One...	*yī zhāng...*	一张...
hard-seat	*yìng zuò*	硬座
hard-sleeper	*yìng wò*	硬卧
soft-sleeper	*ruǎn wò/ruǎn xí*	软卧/软席

I'd like to travel by...	*wǒ xiǎng zuò...*	我想坐...
express train	*tè kuài*	特快
fast train	*kuài chē*	快车
slow train	*màn chē*	慢车
Are there lifts to the platform?	*qù zhàntái yǒu diàntī ma*	去站台有电梯吗?
Can I take my bicycle on the train?	*huǒchē shàng néng dài zìxíngchē ma*	火车上能带自行车吗?
Does this train go to Chengde?	*zhè tàng chē qù chéngdé ma*	这趟车去承德吗?
Is this seat taken?	*zhè ge zuòwèi yǒu rén zuò ma*	这个座位有人坐吗?
May I...	*wǒ kěyǐ.. ma.*	我可以..吗?
open the window?	*kāi chuānghù*	开窗户
smoke?	*chōuyān/xīyān*	抽烟/吸烟
Where are we?	*wǒmen xiànzài zài nǎr*	我们现在在哪儿?
How long does the train stop here?	*huǒchē zài zhèr tíng duō jiǔ*	火车在这儿停多久?
Can you tell me when we get to Tianjin?	*nǐ néng gàosù wǒ jǐ diǎn dào tiānjīn ma*	你能告诉我几点到天津吗?

* buses and coaches

(see **information and tickets**, page 53)

- Every bus and tram has an attendant who sells tickets. Buses and trams usually run between 5am and 11pm. Some buses only run after midnight and the sign 'night bus' is clearly marked on the bus stop.

YOU MAY SEE...

公共汽车总站	*gōnggòng qìchē zǒngzhàn*	bus station
车站	*chē zhàn*	bus stop
快车	*kuài chē*	fast bus
长途车	*chángtú chē*	long-distance coach
夜班车	*yèbān chē*	night bus
禁止通行	*jìnzhǐ tōngxíng*	no entry
请勿吸烟	*qǐng wù xīyān*	no smoking
老弱病残专座	*lǎo ruò bìng cán zhuān zuò*	seats reserved for elderly, the weak, sick and disabled
慢车	*màn chē*	slow bus
电车	*diànchē*	tram

YOU MAY WANT TO SAY...

Where does the bus to the town centre leave from?	去市中心的车从哪儿发车？	*qù shì zhōngxīn de chē cóng nǎr fāchē*
Does the bus to the airport leave from here?	去机场的班车是从这儿发车吗？	*qù jīchǎng de bānchē shì cóng zhèr fāchē ma*
What number is it?	这是几路车？	*zhè shì jǐ lù chē*
Does this bus go to...?	这路车去...吗？	*zhè lù chē qù... ma*
Which stop is it for the museum?	博物馆是哪一站？	*bówùguǎn shì nǎ yī zhàn*
Can you tell me where to get off, please?	你能告诉我在哪儿下车吗？	*nǐ néng gàosù wǒ zài nǎr xià chē ma*
Can you open the doors, please?	请开一下门，好吗？	*qǐng kāi yīxià mén, hǎo ma*

YOU MAY HEAR...

请买票。	*qǐng mǎi piào*	Fare, please.
去市中心的车从这儿发车。	*qù shì zhōng xīn de chē cóng zhèr fāchē*	The bus to the town centre leaves from here.
你在这儿下车吗？	*nǐ zài zhèr xià chē ma*	Are you getting off here?
对不起，我在这儿下车。	*duìbùqǐ, wǒ zài zhèr xià chē*	Excuse me, I'm getting off here.
你坐过头了。	*nǐ zuò guò tóu le*	You've missed the stop.

* underground

(see **information and tickets**, page 53)

YOU MAY SEE...

地铁	*dìtiě*	underground
首车	*shǒu chē*	first train
末车	*mò chē*	last train
升降机/电梯	*shēngjiàngjī/diàntī*	lift
线	*xiàn*	line
通向地面	*tōngxiàng dìmiàn*	to the ground
通向火车	*tōngxiàng huǒchē*	to the train

YOU MAY WANT TO SAY...

Do you have a map of the underground?	你有地铁图吗?	*nǐ yǒu dìtiě tú ma*
Which line is it for the Olympic Games Village?	哪条线是去奥林匹克村的?	*nǎ tiáo xiàn shì qù àolínpǐkè cūn de*
Which stop is it for...?	去...是哪一站?	*qù... shì nǎ yī zhàn*
Is this the right stop for...?	这一站是...吗?	*zhè yī zhàn shì... ma*
Does this train go to...?	这辆车去...吗?	*zhè liàng chē qù... ma*

YOU MAY HEAR...

这是二号线。	*zhè shì èr hào xiàn*	It's line number two.
是下一站。	*shì xià yī zhàn*	It's the next stop.
是上一站。	*shì shàng yī zhàn*	It was the last stop.
你坐错车了。	*nǐ zuò cuò chē le*	You are on the wrong train.

* boats and ferries

(see **information and tickets**, page 53)

YOU MAY SEE...

船	*chuán*	boats
海上航游	*hǎishàng hángyóu*	cruises
轮渡	*lúndù*	ferry
救生艇	*jiùshēng tǐng*	lifeboat
救生衣	*jiùshēng yī*	life jacket
港口	*gǎngkǒu*	port
游船	*yóu chuán*	river trips

YOU MAY WANT TO SAY...

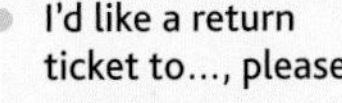

I'd like a return ticket to..., please.	我要一张去...的往返票。	*wǒ yào yī zhāng qù... de wǎngfǎn piào*
Is there a ferry today?	今天有轮渡吗?	*jīntiān yǒu lúnlù ma*

boats and ferries

Are there any boat trips?	有游船吗?	*yǒu yóu chuán ma?*
How long is the cruise?	这个航行要多久?	*zhège hángxíng yào duō jiǔ*
Is there wheelchair access?	有坐轮椅的人的设施吗?	*yǒu zuò lúnyǐ de rén de shèshī ma*
What is the sea like today?	今天的海面状况如何?	*jīntiān de hǎimiàn zhuàngkuàng rúhé*
Is it possible to go out on deck?	有可能到外面的甲板上吗?	*yǒu kě néng dào wàimiàn de jiǎbǎn shàng ma*

YOU MAY HEAR...

...有船	*...yǒu chuán*	boats go on...
每周二和周五	*měi zhōu'èr hé zhōuwǔ*	Tuesdays and Fridays
每隔一天	*měi gé yī tiān*	every other day
海面...	*hǎimiàn...*	the sea is...
平静	*píngjìng*	calm
动荡不定	*dòngdàng bú dìng*	choppy

* hiring cars and bicycles

YOU MAY WANT TO SAY...

I'd like to hire...	*wǒ xiǎng zū...*	我想租...
two bicycles	*liǎng liàng zìxíngchē*	两辆自行车
an automatic car	*yī liàng zìdòng chē*	一辆自动车
For...	*yào zū...*	要租...
one day	*yī tiān*	一天
a week	*yī ge xīngqī*	一个星期
Until...	*zū dào...*	租到...
Friday	*xīngqīwǔ*	星期五
How much is it...	*...duō shǎo qián*	...多少钱?
per day?	*měi tiān*	每天
per week?	*měi xīngqī*	每星期
Is kilometrage/ mileage included?	*hán gōnglǐ shù ma*	含公里数吗?
Is insurance included?	*hán bǎoxiǎn ma*	含保险吗?
My partner wants to drive too.	*wǒde tóngbàn yě xiǎng kāi chē*	我的同伴也想开车。
Is there a deposit?	*yào yājīn ma*	要押金吗?
Can I leave the car...	*wǒ néng bǎ chē tíng zài... ma*	我能把车停在...吗?
at the airport?	*jīchǎng*	机场
in the town centre?	*shì zhōngxīn*	市中心
Can you put the saddle up/down, please?	*qǐng bǎ chēzuò lā gāo/ fàng dī, xíng ma*	请把车座拉高/放低,行吗?

YOU MAY HEAR...

要用多久?	*yào yòng duō jiǔ?*	For how long?
谁是	*shéi shì...*	Who's...
主要开车人?	*zhǔyào kāichērén*	the main driver?
第二开车人?	*dì'èr kāichērén*	the second driver?
请出示你的驾照。	*qǐng chūshì nǐde jiàzhào*	Your driving licence, please.
你想买额外保险吗?	*nǐ xiǎng mǎi éwài bǎoxiǎn ma*	Do you want extra insurance?
一百元押金。	*yī bǎi yuán yājīn*	There's a deposit of 100 yuan.
还车时请加满油。	*huán chē shí qǐng jiāmǎn yóu*	Please return the car with a full tank.
请六点前还车/自行车。	*qǐng liù diǎn qián huán chē/ zìxíngchē*	Please return the car/bicycle before six o'clock.

* driving

In China, you drive on the right. Driving can be difficult due to the volume of traffic, with no special lanes for buses, taxis or bikes.

YOU MAY SEE...

停车场	*tíngchē chǎng*	car park
自行车道	*zìxíngchē dào*	bicycle path
当心	*dāngxīn*	caution
危险	*wéixiǎn*	danger
危险弯道	*wéixiǎn wāndào*	dangerous bend
绕道走	*ràodào zǒu*	diversion
高速公路终止	*gāosù gōnglù zhōngzhǐ*	end of motorway
出口	*chūkǒu*	exit
急救站	*jíjiùzhàn*	first-aid post
车行	*chē háng*	garage
让行	*ràng xíng*	give way
右行	*yòu xíng*	keep right
火车栅栏	*huǒchē shānlán*	level crossing
最高车速	*zuìgāo chēsù*	maximum speed limit
高速公路	*gāosù gōnglù*	motorway
不许超车	*bù xǔ chāochē*	no overtaking
不许停车	*bù xǔ tíngchē*	no parking
此路不通	*cǐ lù bùtōng*	no through road
单行线	*dānxíng xiàn*	one-way street
道路关闭	*dàolù guānbì*	road closed
正在修路	*zhèng zài xiūlù*	road works
必须系安全带	*bìxū jì ānquán dài*	seatbelt compulsory
服务区/加油站	*fúwù qū/ jiāyóu zhàn*	service/petrol station
路面湿滑	*lùmiàn shīhuá*	slippery surface
慢	*màn*	slow

停	*tíng*	stop
息火	*xí huǒ*	switch your engine off
开前灯	*kāi qiándēng*	use headlights

YOU MAY WANT TO SAY...

Where is the nearest petrol station?	最近的加油站在哪儿?	*zuìjìn de jiāyóu zhàn zài nǎr*
Fill it up with...	加满...	*jiā mǎn...*
unleaded	不含铅的油	*bù hánqiān de yóu*
diesel	柴油	*cháiyóu*
200 yuan worth of unleaded, please.	请加值两百元不含铅的油。	*qǐng jiā zhí liǎng bǎi yuán bù hánqiān de yóu*
20 litres of super unleaded, please.	请加二十升高级不含铅的油。	*qǐng jiā èrshí shēng gāojí bù hánqiān de yóu*
A can of oil, please.	请来一罐油。	*qǐng lái yī guàn yóu*
Can you check the tyre pressure, please?	能给我检查一下轮胎压吗?	*néng gěi wǒ jiǎnchá yīxià lúntāi yā ma*
Can you change the tyre, please?	能换轮胎吗?	*néng huàn lúntāi ma*
Where is the air, please?	气压在哪儿?	*qì yā zài nǎr*

YOU MAY HEAR...

你要什么？	*nǐ yào shénme*	What would you like?
你要多少？	*nǐ yào duō shǎo*	How much do you want?
请给我钥匙。	*qǐng gěi wǒ yàoshi.*	The key, please.

* mechanical problems

YOU MAY WANT TO SAY...

My car has broken down.	我的车坏了。	*wǒde chē huài le*
I've run out of petrol.	我没有油了。	*wǒ méiyǒu yóu le*
I have a puncture.	我的车胎被扎破了。	*wǒde chētāi bèi zhā pò le*
Can you telephone a garage?	你能给车行打个电话吗？	*nǐ néng gěi chēháng dǎ ge diànhuà ma*
Do you do repairs?	你们修理车吗？	*nǐmen xiūlǐ chē ma*
I don't know what's wrong.	我不知道哪儿坏了。	*wǒ bù zhīdào nǎr huài le*
I think it's the...	我觉得是...的问题	*wǒ juéde shì...de wèntí*
clutch	挡	*dǎng*
I need a...	我需要一个...	*wǒ xūyào yī ge...*
The ... doesn't work.	这个...不行	*zhè ge...bù xíng*
Is it serious?	严重吗？	*yánzhòng ma*

car parts

Can you repair it today?	今天能修好吗？	*jīntiān néng xiū hǎo ma*
When will it be ready?	什么时候能修好？	*shénme shíhòu néng xiū hǎo*
How much will it cost?	要多少钱？	*yào duō shǎo qián*

YOU MAY HEAR...

哪儿坏了/出问题了？	*nǎr huài le/ chū wèntí le*	What's wrong with it?
我没有你需要的零件。	*wǒ méi yǒu nǐ xūyào de língjiàn*	I don't have the necessary parts.
下周二再来。	*xià zhōu'èr zài lái*	Come back next Tuesday.
...能修好。	*...néng xiū hǎo*	It'll be ready...
一个小时后	*yī ge xiǎoshí hòu*	in an hour
星期一	*xīngqīyī*	on Monday
一共...钱	*yīgòng... qián*	It'll cost...

* car parts

YOU MAY WANT TO SAY...

accelerator	油门	*yóumén*
alternator	交流发电器	*jiāoliú fādiàn qì*
back tyre	后轮胎	*hòu lúntāi*
battery	电池	*diànchí*

bonnet	引擎盖	*yǐnqíng gài*
brakes	刹车	*shāchē*
carburettor	化油器	*huàyóu qì*
distributor	配电器	*pèidiàn qì*
engine	发动机	*fādòng jī*
exhaust pipe	排气管	*páiqì guǎn*
fanbelt	风扇皮带	*fēngshàn pídài*
fuel gauge	油量计/油表	*yóuliàng jì/ yóubiǎo*
gear box	变速器	*biànsù qì*
gears	挡	*dǎng*
headlights	前灯	*qián dēng*
ignition	点火装置	*diǎnhuǒ zhuāngzhì*
indicator	转向灯	*zhuǎnxiàng dēng*
radiator	暖气	*nuǎnqì*
rear lights	尾灯	*wěi dēng*
reversing lights	倒车灯	*dàochē dēng*
side lights	侧灯	*cè dēng*
spare tyre	备用轮胎	*bèiyòng lúntāi*
spark plugs	火花塞	*huǒhuā sāi*
starter motor	启动器	*qǐdòng qì*
windscreen	挡风玻璃	*dǎngfēng bōlí*
windscreen wiper	刮雨器	*guāyǔ qì*

✻ bicycle parts

YOU MAY WANT TO SAY...

back light	后灯	*hòu dēng*
chain	链条	*liàntiáo*
frame	框架	*kuāngjià*
front light	前灯	*qián dēng*
gears	变速器	*biànsùqì*
handlebars	扶手	*fú shǒu*
inner tube	内带	*nèi dài*
pump	气筒	*qìtǒng*
saddle	车座	*chēzuò*
spokes	车轮辐条	*chēlún fútiáo*
tyre	轮胎	*lúntāi*
valve	气门心	*qìménxīn*
wheel	车轮子	*chēlúnzi*

accommodation

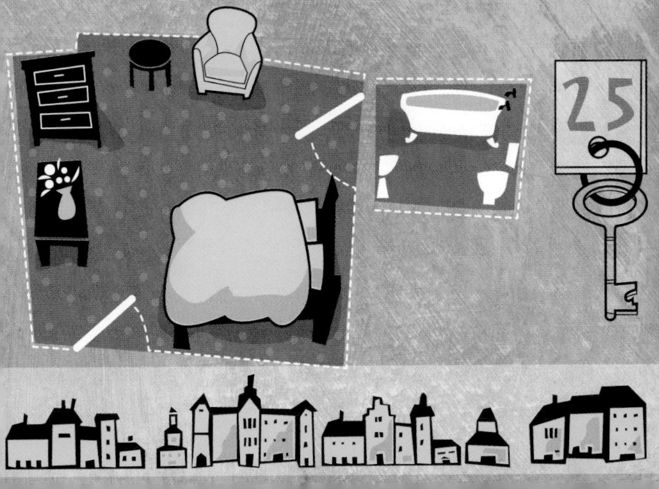

* accommodation

- The Chinese use the American system for counting floors, e.g. the English ground floor is the first floor in Chinese, the first floor is the second floor, etc.

YOU MAY SEE...

请勿打扰	*qǐng wù dǎrǎo*	do not disturb
饮用水	*yǐnyòng shuǐ*	drinking water
值班经理	*zhíbān jīnglǐ*	duty manager
一层	*yī céng*	ground floor
宾馆	*bīn guǎn*	guest house
饭店/酒店	*fàndiàn/jiǔdiàn*	hotel
旅店	*lǚdiàn*	inn
洗衣房	*xǐyīfáng*	laundry
电梯	*diàntī*	lift
前台	*qiántái*	reception
餐厅	*cāntīng*	restaurant
房间服务	*fángjiān fúwù*	room service
男	*nán*	toilets (male)
女	*nǚ*	toilets (female)

* booking in advance

(see **telephones**, page 143; **the internet**, page 147)

YOU MAY WANT TO SAY...

Do you have a...	你有... 吗?	*nǐ yǒu... ma*
single room?	单人房间	*dānrén fángjiān*
double room?	双人房间	*shuāngrén fángjiān*
twin-bedded room?	两个单人床的房间	*liǎng gè dānrén chuáng defángjiān*
For...	要...	*yào...*
two nights	两个晚上	*liǎng ge wǎnshàng*
a week	一个星期	*yī ge xīngqī*
From... to...	从...到	*cóng... dào*
Only for tonight.	只要今晚	*zhīyào jīnwǎn*
With...	带...	*dài...*
bath	浴缸	*yùgāng*
shower	淋浴	*línyù*
How much is it...	多少钱...	*duō shǎo qián...*
per night?	一天?	*yī tiān*
Is breakfast included?	含早餐吗?	*hán zǎocān ma*
Is there a reduction for children?	孩子减价吗?	*háizi jiǎnjià ma*
Do you have...	你有...吗?	*nǐ yǒu... ma*
anything cheaper?	便宜一些的	*piányí yīxiē de*
a website?	网站	*wǎngzhàn*

booking in advance

Can I pay by...	我能付...吗?	*wǒ néng fù... ma*
credit card?	信用卡	*xìnyòng kǎ*
Can I book online?	我能在网上订吗?	*wǒ néng zài wǎngshàng dìng ma*

YOU MAY HEAR...

我能帮助你吗?	*wǒ néng bāngzhù nǐ ma*	Can I help you?
你想什么时候住?	*nǐ xiǎng shénme shíhòu zhù*	When do you want to come?
要住几晚?	*yào zhù jǐ wǎn*	For how many nights?
多少人?	*duō shǎo rén*	For how many people?
单间还是双间?	*dānjiān háishì shuāngjiān*	Single or double room?
要双人床吗?	*yào shuāngrén chuáng ma*	Do you want a double bed?
带...	*dài...*	With...
浴缸	*yùgāng*	bath
淋浴	*línyù*	shower
您贵姓?	*nín guì xìng*	What's your surname, please?
你叫什么?	*nǐ jiào shénme*	What's your name, please?
你有信用卡吗?	*nǐ yǒu xìnyòng kǎ ma*	Do you have a credit card?

三百元一天，含早餐。	*sānbǎi yuán yī tiān, hán zǎocān*	It's 300 yuan per night, including breakfast
对不起，我们满员。	*duìbùqǐ, wǒmen mǎnyuán*	I'm sorry, we're full.

* checking in

YOU MAY WANT TO SAY...

I have a reservation for...	我预订了 ... 的房间。	*wǒ yùdìng le... de fángjiān*
tonight	今晚	*jīnwǎn*
It's in the name of...	是以...的名字订的。	*shì yǐ... de míngzì dìng de*
I'm paying by credit card.	我用信用卡支付。	*wǒ yòng xìnyòngkǎ zhīfù*

YOU MAY HEAR...

你预订房间/公寓了吗?	*nǐ yùdìng fángjiān/gōngyù le ma*	Have you reserved a room/an apartment?
要住几晚/几天?	*yào zhù jǐ wǎn/jǐ tiān*	For how many nights?
您贵姓?	*nín guì xìng*	What's your surname?
看一下你的护照，可以吗?	*kàn yīxià nǐde hùzhào, kěyǐ ma*	Can I have your passport, please?
我能刷一下你的信用卡吗?	*wǒ néng shuā yīxià nǐde xìnyòng kǎ ma*	Can I take a copy of your credit card?

REGISTRATION CARD INFORMATION...

姓	*xìng*	surname
名	*míng*	name
家庭住址	*jiātíng zhùzhǐ*	home address
邮编	*yóubiān*	postcode
国籍	*guójí*	nationality
职业	*zhíyè*	occupation
出生日期	*chūshēng rìqī*	date of birth
出生地点	*chūshēng dìdiǎn*	place of birth
护照号码	*hùzhào hàomǎ*	passport number
从何处来	*cóng héchǔ lái*	coming from
去往何处	*qùwǎng héchǔ*	going to
日期	*rìqī*	date
签名	*qiānmíng*	signature

* hotels, inns and hostels

YOU MAY WANT TO SAY...

- Where can I park? 我能在哪儿停车? *wǒ néng zài nǎr tíng chē*
- Do you have... 你们有...吗? *nǐmen yǒu... ma*
  a cot for the baby? 婴儿床 *yīng'ér chuáng*
- What time is breakfast? 早餐是几点? *zǎocān shì jǐ diǎn*
- Where is... ...在哪儿? *...zài nǎr*
  the bar? 酒吧 *jiǔbā*

Is there...	这儿有...吗?	*zhèr yǒu...ma*
an internet connection?	互联网接口	*hùliánwǎng jiēkǒu*

YOU MAY HEAR...

停车场在...	*tíngchē chǎng zài...*	The car park is...
饭店的地下	*fàndiàn de dìxià*	under the hotel
不好意思，我们今晚没有空房间了。	*bù hǎo yìsi, wǒmen jīnwǎn méi yǒu kōng fángjiān le*	I'm afraid we don't have any rooms available tonight.
也许明天能给你换房间。	*yěxǔ míngtiān néng gěi nǐ huàn fángjiān*	We might be able to change your room tomorrow.
早餐从...到...。	*zǎocān cóng... dào...*	Breakfast is from... to...
请跟我来，我告诉你餐厅/酒吧在哪儿。	*qǐng gēn wǒ lái, wǒ gàosù nǐ cān tīng/ jiǔbā zài nǎr*	Follow me, I'll show you where the dining room/bar is.
房间服务从...到...。	*fángjiān fúwù cóng... dào...*	There's room service from... to...
...有互联网接口。	*...yǒu hùliánwǎng jiēkǒu*	There's an internet connection...
你的房间里	*nǐde fángjiān lǐ*	in your room.

* requests and queries

YOU MAY WANT TO SAY...

Are there any messages for me?	有给我的留言条吗?	*yǒu gěi wǒde liúyán tiáo ma*
I'm expecting...	我等...	*wǒ děng...*
a phone call	一个电话	*yī ge diànhuà*
a fax	一份传真	*yī fèn chuánzhēn*
Can I...	我能...吗?	*wǒ néng....ma*
leave this in the safe?	把这个留在保险箱里	*bǎ zhège liú zài bǎoxiǎnxiāng lǐ*
put it on my room bill?	把这个算在我的房费里	*bǎ zhège suàn zài wǒde fángfèi lǐ*
Can you...	你能不能...	*nǐ néng bù néng...*
give me my things from the safe?	把我的东西从保险箱里取出?	*bǎ wǒde dōngxī cóng bǎoxiǎnxiāng lǐ qǔ chū*
wake me up at eight o'clock?	八点叫醒我?	*bā diǎn jiào xǐng wǒ*
order me a taxi?	替我叫一辆出租?	*tì wǒ jiào yī liàng chūzū chē*
Do you have...	你们有没有...	*nǐmen yǒu méi yǒu...*
a baby alarm?	婴儿监护器?	*yīng'ér jiānhùqì*
I need another pillow.	我还要一个枕头.	*wǒ hái yào yī ge zhěntóu*
I need...	我需要...	*wǒ xūyào...*
an adaptor	转换插头。	*zhuǎnhuàn chātóu*
I've lost my key.	我的钥匙丢了。	*wǒde yàoshi diū le*

YOU MAY HEAR...

没有，没有您的留言。	*méi yǒu, méi yǒu nínde liúyán*	No, there are no messages for you.
您需要叫醒服务吗?	*nín xūyào jiào xǐng fúwù ma*	Do you want a wake up call?
几点?	*jǐ diǎn*	(For) what time?
请等一下。	*qǐng děng yīxià*	Just a moment, please.

✻ problems and complaints

YOU MAY WANT TO SAY...

Excuse me.	对不起。	*duìbùqǐ*
The room is...	我的房间...	*wǒde fángjiān...*
too hot	太热	*tài rè*
too cold	太冷	*tài lěng*
too small	太小	*tài xiǎo*
too noisy	太吵	*tài chǎo*
There isn't/aren't any...	没有...	*méi yǒu...*
toilet paper	卫生纸	*wèishēng zhǐ*
hot water	热水	*rè shuǐ*
electricity	电	*diàn*
towels	毛巾	*máojīn*
I can't open the window.	我打不开窗户。	*wǒ dǎ bù kāi chuānghù*
I can't switch on the TV.	我关不掉电视。	*wǒ guān bū diào diànshì*

problems and complaints

The bathroom is dirty.	卫生间脏/不干净。	*wèishēngjiān zàng/ bù gānjìng*
The toilet doesn't flush.	厕所不冲水。	*cèsuǒ bù chōngshuǐ*
The key doesn't work.	钥匙开不开。	*yàoshi kāi bù kāi*
The shower is not working.	淋浴出问题了。	*línyù chū wèntí le*
I want to see the manager!	我要见经理!	*wǒ yào jiàn jīnglǐ*

YOU MAY HEAR...

请稍等。	*qǐng shāo děng*	Just a moment, please.
当然可以。	*dāngrán kěyǐ*	Of course.
我马上给你再送去一个。	*wǒ mǎshàng gěi nǐ zài sòng qù yī gè*	I'll bring you another one immediately.
我明天为你修理。	*wǒ míngtiān wéi nǐ xiūlǐ*	I'll fix it for you tomorrow.
对不起，今天不行了。	*duìbùqǐ, jīntiān bù xíng le*	I'm sorry, it's not possible today.
对不起，我无能为力。	*duìbùqǐ, wǒ wú néng wéi lì*	I'm sorry, there's nothing I can do.
我们对此不负责。	*wǒmen duì cǐ bú fùzé*	We aren't responsible.

* checking out

YOU MAY WANT TO SAY...

I'd like to...	我想…	*wǒ xiǎng…*
pay the bill and check out	结帐并办理离店手续	*jiézhàng bìng bànlǐ lídiàn shǒuxù*
stay another night	再住一个晚上	*zài zhù yī ge wǎnshàng*
What time is check out?	几点办理离店手续?	*jǐ diǎn bànlǐ lídiàn shǒuxù*
Can I...	我能不能…	*wǒ néng bù néng…*
have a late check out?	晚一些办理离店手续?	*wǎn yīxiē bànlǐ lídiàn shǒuxù*
leave my luggage here?	把我的行李留在这儿?	*bǎ wǒde xínglǐ liú zài zhèr*
There's a mistake in the bill.	帐单里有个错。	*zhàngdān lǐ yǒu ge cuò*
I/We've had a great time here.	我/我们在这儿过得很愉快。	*wǒ/ wǒmen zài zhèr guò de hěn yúkuài*

YOU MAY HEAR

房间可以用到…	*fángjiān kěyǐ yòng dào…*	You can have the room till…
多少件行李?	*duō shǎo jiàn xínglǐ*	How many bags?
留在这儿。	*liú zài zhèr*	Leave them here.
让我查查。	*ràng wǒ chácha*	Let me check it.
请再光临!	*qǐng zài guānglín*	Come again!

* self-catering/serviced apartments

(see **problems and complaints**, page 83)

YOU MAY WANT TO SAY...

Where is...	...在哪儿?	*... zài nǎr*
the fusebox?	保险丝盒	*bǎoxiǎnsī hé*
How does the... work?	怎么...?	*zěnme...*
hot water	操作热水	*cāozuò rè shuǐ*
Is there...	有 ...吗?	*yǒu...ma*
air-conditioning?	空调	*kōngtiáo*
Can I borrow...	我能借一下...吗?	*wǒ néng jiè yīxià...ma*
a corkscrew?	螺丝刀	*luósīdāo*
We need...	我们需要...	*wǒmen xūyào...*
a plumber	水暖工	*shuǐnuǎngōng*
an electrician	电工	*diàngōng*
How can I contact you?	我怎么和你联络?	*wǒ zěnme hé nǐ liánluò*

YOU MAY HEAR...

说明书在炉子/锅炉旁边。	*shuōmíngshū zài lúzi/ guōlú pángbiān*	The instructions are by the cooker/boiler.
在柜子里有多余的毯子/枕头。	*zài guìzi lǐ yǒu duōyú de tǎnzi/zhěntóu*	There are spare blankets/pillows in the cupboard.
我的手机号是...	*wǒde shǒujī hào shì...*	My mobile number is...

food&drink

● There are regional differences in Chinese cuisine. For example, Sichuan food is famous for its use of chilli and pepper, while Cantonese food emphasises freshness, and the flavour is rather mild. Evening food markets are worth visiting, where you buy from food-stalls in the street.

YOU MAY SEE...

酒吧	*jiǔbā*	bar
烧烤	*shāokǎo*	barbecue/grill
粤菜	*yuè cài*	cantonese food
咖啡厅	*kāfēi tīng*	coffee bar
饺子馆	*jiǎozi guǎn*	dumpling restaurant
夜市	*yè shì*	evening food market
快餐	*kuài cān*	fast food
冰淇淋店/冷饮店	*bīngqílín diàn/lěngyǐn diàn*	ice cream parlour
铺子	*pùzi*	kiosk
面馆	*miàn guǎn*	noodle bar
餐馆/酒楼	*cānguǎn/jiǔlóu*	restaurant
烤鸭店	*kǎoyā diàn*	roast duck restaurant
海鲜店/海鲜城	*hǎixiān diàn/hǎixiān chéng*	seafood restaurant
自助餐	*zìzhù cān*	self-service
套餐	*tào cān*	set menu
川菜	*chuān cài*	Sichuan food
快餐店	*kuàicān diàn*	snack bar
茶馆	*cháguǎn*	tearoom

* making bookings

YOU MAY WANT TO SAY...

I'd like to reserve a table for...	我想预订一张桌子，...	wǒ xiǎng yùdìng yī zhāng zhuōzi, ...
two people	两个人	liǎng ge rén
two adults and three children	两个大人，三个小孩	liǎng ge dàrén, sān ge xiǎo hái
tomorrow evening at half past eight	明天晚上八点半	míngtiān wǎnshàng bādiǎn bàn
this evening at nine o'clock	今天晚上九点	jīntiān wǎnshàng jiǔ diǎn
My name is...	我叫...	wǒ jiào...
Could you get us a table...	你能... 给我们一个桌吗?	nǐ néng... gěi wǒmen yī ge zhuō ma
earlier?	早一些	zǎo yīxiē
later?	晚一些	wǎn yīxiē

YOU MAY HEAR...

你几点要桌?	nǐ jǐ diǎn yào zhuō	What time would you like the table for?
几个人?/几位?	jǐ ge rén/jǐ wèi	For how many people?
你叫什么?	nǐ jiào shénme	What's your name?
对不起，我们订满了。	duìbùqǐ, wǒmen dìng mǎn le	I'm sorry we're fully booked.

* at the restaurant

YOU MAY WANT TO SAY...

I've booked a table.	我订了一个桌。	*wǒ dìng le yī ge zhuō*
We haven't booked.	我们没有订桌。	*wǒmen méi yǒu dìng zhuō*
Have you got a table for four, please?	你有四人桌吗?	*nǐ yǒu sì rén zhuō ma*
Have you got a high chair?	有儿童高椅子吗?	*yǒu értóng gāo yǐzi ma*
How long's the wait?	要等多久?	*yào děng duō jiǔ*
Can we wait here?	我们能在这儿等吗?	*wǒmen néng zài zhèr děng ma*
Do you take credit cards?	你们收信用卡吗?	*nǐmen shōu xìnyòng kǎ ma*

YOU MAY HEAR...

欢迎光临!	*huānyíng guānglín*	Welcome!
你预订桌了吗?	*nǐ yùdìng zhuō le ma*	Have you got a reservation?
吸烟还是不吸烟?	*xīyān háishì bù xīyān*	Smoking or non-smoking?
请稍等.	*qǐng shāo děng*	Just a moment, please.

你愿意等吗?	*nǐ yuànyì děng ma*	**Would you like to wait?**
对不起，我们...	*duìbùqǐ, wǒmen...*	**I'm sorry we're...**
满员了	*mǎnyuán le*	**full**
关门了	*guānmén le*	**closed**
我们(不)收信用卡。	*wǒmen(bù) shōu xìnyòng kǎ*	**We (don't) accept credit cards.**

✱ ordering your food

Please note that Chinese restaurants do not have special children's menus. Usually, all dishes are served at the same time and are shared. Or you can start with some cold dishes followed by hot dishes (in terms of temperature). There's no separate course for dessert. Most restaurants won't serve coffee.

YOU MAY WANT TO SAY...

Excuse me!	对不起!	*duìbùqǐ*
The menu, please.	请拿菜单来	*qǐng ná càidān lái*
Do you have...	你们有...吗?	*nǐmen yǒu... ma*
vegetarian food?	素食	*sù shí*
a set menu?	套餐	*tào cān*
Is it self-service?	这是自助餐吗?	*zhè shì zì hù cān ma*
We're ready to order.	我们可以点了。	*wǒmen kě ǐ diǎn le*
Can I have...?	我要...	*wǒ yào...*

I'd like... for starters.	凉菜/头盘要...	*liáng cài/tóupán yào...*
I'd like... for the main course.	热菜/正餐要...	*rè cài/zhèngcān yào...*
I'd like... followed by...	先上 ...再上...	*xiān shàng... zài shàng...*
Does that come with vegetables?	那个配有蔬菜吗?	*nà gè pèi yǒu shūcài ma*
What's this please?	请问, 这是什么?	*qǐng wèn, zhè shì shénme*
What are today's specials?	今天的特菜是什么?	*jīntiān de tècài shì shénme*
What's the local speciality?	本地的风味是什么?	*běndì de fēngwèi shì shénme*
I'd like it rare/medium/well done, please.	我喜欢做得嫩一些/适中/老一些。	*wǒ xǐhuān zuò de nèn yīxiē/shìzhōng/lǎo yīxiē*
Please will you bring some...	请给我们一点...	*qǐng gěi wǒmen yīdiǎn...*
soya sauce?	酱油?	*jiàngyóu*
salt and pepper?	盐和胡椒?	*yán hé hújiāo*
Excuse me, I've changed my mind.	对不起, 我改变主意了。	*duìbùqǐ, wǒ gǎibiàn zhǔyì le*

YOU MAY HEAR...

您想先喝一些什么吗?	*nín xiǎng xiān hē yīxiē shénme ma*	**Would you like a drink first?**
您要点菜吗?	*nín yào diǎn cài ma*	**Are you ready to order?**
您要凉菜/头盘吗?	*nín yào liáng cài/ tóupán ma*	**Would you like to have some cold dishes/starters?**
要什么热菜?	*yào shénme rè cài*	**What would you like for the main course?**
我们推荐...	*wǒmen tuījiàn...*	**We recommend...**
对不起，那个没有了。	*duìbùqǐ, nàge méi yǒu le*	**I'm sorry, that's finished.**
还要别的吗?	*hái yào biéde ma*	**Anything else?**
这个菜您要怎么做?	*zhè ge cài nín yào zěnme zuò*	**How would you like it cooked?**
您想看一下酒水单吗?	*nín xiǎng kàn yīxià jiǔ shuǐ dān ma*	**Would you like to see the wine and beverage list?**
您想要茶吗?	*nín xiǎng yào chá ma*	**Would you like some tea?**

The Chinese equivalent of 'Yes, please.' in response to 'Would you like some tea?' is 'want, thank you' 想，谢谢 (*xiǎng, xièxie*) as the word 'please' 请 (*qǐng*) is never used for this purpose.

* ordering your drinks

● 酒 (*jiǔ*) refers to all types of alcoholic drinks including spirits, wine and beer. Most Chinese people like sweet wine better than dry wine, and red is more popular than white. (see drinks under **menu reader**, page 104)

YOU MAY WANT TO SAY...

● **Can we see the wine and drinks list, please?**	我们能看一下酒水单吗?	*wǒmen néng kàn yīxià jiǔ shuǐ dān ma*
● **A bottle of this please.**	来一瓶这个。	*lái yī píng zhège*
● **A glass of the... please.**	请来一杯...	*qǐng lái yī bēi...*
● **We'll have the red/white wine, please.**	我们要红/白葡萄酒。	*wǒmen yào hóng/bái pútáojiǔ*
● **What beers do you have?**	你们有什么啤酒?	*nǐmen yǒu shénme píjiǔ*
● **Is that a bottle or draught?**	是瓶装还是鲜啤酒?	*shì píngzhuāng háishì xiān píjiǔ*
● **What wines do you have?**	你们有什么葡萄酒?	*nǐmen yǒu shénme pútáojiǔ*
● **Is there a local wine?**	有本地葡萄酒吗?	*yǒu běndì pútáojiǔ ma*
● **Can I have...**	我要一个..., 行吗?	*wǒ yào yī ge..., xíng ma*
a gin and tonic?	金酒及汤力水	*jīnjiǔ jí tānglìshuǐ*
a whisky?	威士忌	*wēishìjì*

Do you have any liqueurs?	你有力娇甜酒吗?	*nǐ yǒu lìjiāo tián jiǔ ma*
A bottle of mineral water, please.	来一瓶矿泉水。	*lái yī píng kuàngquán shuǐ*
What soft drinks do you have?	你们有什么软饮料?	*nǐmen yǒu shénme ruǎn yǐnliào*

YOU MAY HEAR...

要冰和柠檬吗?	*yào bīng hé níngméng ma*	Ice and lemon?
带汽的水还是不带汽的?	*dàiqìde shuǐ háishì bù dàiqìde*	Sparkling or still water?
大瓶还是小瓶?	*dà píng háishì xiǎo píng*	A large or small bottle?

* bars and tea-rooms

- There are various snacks you can order to go together with your drink or pot of tea. They range from savoury food to sweet cakes.

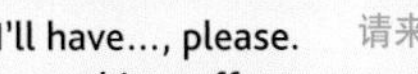

YOU MAY WANT TO SAY...

I'll have..., please.	请来...	*qǐng lái...*
a white coffee	一个白咖啡	*yī ge bái kāfēi*
a black coffee	一个黑咖啡	*yī ge hēi kāfēi*
a pot of tea	一壶茶	*yī hú chá*
a fruit tea	一个果茶	*yī ge guǒ chá*

With milk/lemon	加牛奶/鲜柠檬	*jiā niú nǎi/xiān níngméng*
A glass of... wine apple juice	一杯... 葡萄酒 苹果汁	*yī bēi...* *pútáo jiǔ* *píngguǒ zhī*
No ice, thanks.	不要冰，谢谢。	*bú yào bīng, xièxie*
A bottle of water, please.	请来一瓶水。	*qǐng lái yī píng shuǐ*
A piece of chocolate cake, please.	请来一块巧克力蛋糕。	*qǐng lái yī kuài qiǎokèlì dàngāo*
A plate of snacks, please.	请来一盘小吃。	*qǐng lái yī pán xiǎochī*
Same again please.	再来一份。	*zài lái yīfèn*
How much is that?	那个多少钱?	*nàge duō shǎo qián*

YOU MAY HEAR...

欢迎光临！	*huānyíng guānglín*	Welcome!
您要什么?	*nín yào shénme*	What would you like?
大的还是小的?	*dàde háishì xiǎode*	Large or small?
加冰吗?	*jiā bīng ma*	With ice?
马上就来。	*mǎshàng jiù lái*	Right away.

* comments and requests

YOU MAY WANT TO SAY...

This is delicious!	太好吃了!	*tài hǎochī le*
Can I/we have more... water, please?	我/我们能不能再要一些... 水?	*wǒ/wǒmen néng bù néng zài yào yīxiē... shuǐ*
Can I/we have... please?	请再给我/我们...	*qǐng zài gěi wǒ/ wǒmen...*
another bottle of wine	一瓶葡萄酒	*yī píng pútáojiǔ*
another glass	一个杯子	*yī ge bēizi*
I can't eat another thing.	我一点儿都吃不下了。	*wǒ yīdiǎnr dōu chī bū xiàle*

YOU MAY HEAR...

慢慢用。	*mànman yòng*	Enjoy your meal.
没问题吧?	*méi wèntí ba*	Is everything all right?
您吃得好吗?	*nín chīde hǎo ma*	Did you enjoy your meal?

* special requirements

YOU MAY WANT TO SAY...

I'm diabetic.	我有糖尿病。	*wǒ yǒu tángniàobìng*
I'm vegetarian.	我吃素。	*wǒ chīsù*

I'm allergic to...	我对... 过敏。	*wǒ duì... guòmǐn*
nuts	果仁	*guǒrén*
cow's milk	牛奶	*niú nǎi*
MSG	味精	*wèijīng*
shellfish	带壳的海鲜	*dàiké de hǎixiān*
I don't eat meat or fish.	我不吃肉和鱼。	*wǒ bù chī ròu hé yú*
I'm vegan.	我是严格的素食者。	*wǒ shì yángé de sùshízhě*
I can't eat...	我不能吃...	*wǒ bù néng chī...*
dairy products	奶制品	*nǎi zhìpǐn*
wheat products	大麦类食品	*dàmài lèi shípǐn*
Do you have... food?	你们有...食品吗?	*nǐmen yǒu... shípǐn ma*
halal	清真	*qīngzhēn*
free-range	自由放养的家禽	*zìyóu fàngyǎngde jiāqín*
low sodium	低钠	*dī nà*
low fat	低脂肪	*dī zhīfáng*
organic	绿色	*lǜsè*
Do you have anything without meat?	你们有不放肉的食品吗?	*nǐmen yǒu bù fàng ròu de shípǐn ma*
Is that cooked with...	那里面放...了吗?	*nà lǐmiàn fàng... le ma*
garlic?	大蒜	*dàsuàn*
nuts?	果仁	*guǒrén*
Does that have nuts in it?	那里面含果仁吗?	*nà lǐmiàn hán guǒrén ma*

YOU MAY HEAR...

我去问问厨房。	*wǒ qù wènwen chúfáng*	I'll check with the kitchen.
都有…	*dōu yǒu…*	It's all got… in it.
黄豆	*huáng dòu*	soya beans
大蒜	*dàsuàn*	garlic
果仁	*guǒrén*	nuts

* problems and complaints

YOU MAY WANT TO SAY...

This is…	这个…	*zhège…*
cold	凉了	*liáng le*
underdone	没熟	*méi shóu*
burnt	焦了	*jiāo le*
I didn't order this.	我没有点这个。	*wǒ méi yǒu diǎn zhège*
I ordered the…	我点的是 …	*wǒ diǎn de shì…*
Is our food coming soon?	我们点的是不是快来了?	*wǒmen diǎnde shì bú shì kuàilái le*

* paying the bill

- No tipping is expected in restaurants. Service is normally included in the bill. Culturally, it is not acceptable to divide the bill.

YOU MAY WANT TO SAY...

The bill, please.	买单/请结帐。	*mǎi dān/qǐng jiézhàng*
Is service included?	含服务费吗?	*hán fúwùfèi ma*
There's a mistake here.	这儿有个错。	*zhèr yǒu ge cuò*
That was fantastic, thank you.	简直太好了，谢谢。	*jiǎnzhí tàihǎo le, xièxie*

YOU MAY HEAR...

对不起，我们只收现金。	*duìbùqǐ, wǒmen zhǐ shōu xiànjīn*	**Sorry, we only accept cash.**
你要收据吗?	*nǐ yào shōujù ma*	**Do you want a receipt?**

* buying food

YOU MAY WANT TO SAY...

I'd like... please.	我要...	*wǒ yào...*
some of those/ that	一些那种东西/这个	*yīxiē nàzhǒng dōngxī/zhège*
a kilo (of...)	一公斤	*yī gōngjīn*
half a kilo (of...)	半公斤	*bàn gōngjīn*
200g of that	两百克那个	*liǎng bǎi kè nàge*
a piece of that	一片那个	*yī piàn nàge*
two slices of that	两片那个	*liǎng piàn nàge*
How much is...	...多少钱?	*duō shǎo qián*
that?	那个	*nàge*
a kilo of lychees?	一公斤荔枝	*yī gōngjīn lìzhī*
What's that, please?	那是什么?	*nà shì shénme*
Have you got...	有...吗?	*yǒu... ma*
any yoghurt?	酸奶	*suānnǎi*
any bread?	面包	*miànbāo*
A bit more/less please.	再多一些 /少一些。	*zài duō yīxiē/shǎo yīxiē*
That's enough, thank you.	够了，谢谢。	*gòu le, xièxie*
That's all, thank you.	就要这么多，谢谢。	*jiù yào zhème duō, xièxie*
Can I have a bag please?	能给我一个袋子吗?	*néng gěi wǒ yī ge dàizi ma*

YOU MAY HEAR...

你需要帮助吗？	*nǐ xūyào bāngzhù ma*	Can I help you?
你要什么？	*nǐ yào shénme*	What would you like?
你要多少？	*nǐ yào duō shǎo*	How much would you like?
你要几个？	*nǐ yào jǐ gè*	How many would you like?
还要别的吗？	*hái yào biéde ma*	Anything else?

* eating with a Chinese family

- If you get invited to a Chinese home for meal, it's polite to turn up 10 to 15 minutes before the agreed time. During the meal, the host or hostess will automatically put food on your plate or bowl, and refill your glass as soon as it is empty, otherwise, they feel that are not looking after their guests properly.

YOU MAY WANT TO SAY...

Thank you for inviting me to your house.	谢谢你请我来你家。	*xièxie nǐ qǐng wǒ lái nǐ jiā*
It smells delicious.	太香了。	*tài xiāng le*
Your food is just wonderful.	你的饭好极了。	*nǐde fàn hǎojíle*
I've had enough.	我吃饱了。	*wǒ chī bǎo le*

Seriously, I can't have any more.	真的，我实在吃不下了。	*zhēnde, wǒ shízài chī bù xià le*
Sorry, I can't use chopsticks.	对不起，我不会用筷子。	*duìbùqǐ, wǒ bū huì yòng kuàizi*
Do you have knives and forks?	你们有刀叉吗?	*nǐmen yǒu dāo chā ma*

YOU MAY HEAR...

菜不多。	*cài bù duō*	There aren't enough dishes.
我做饭做得不好。	*wǒ zuòfàn zuò de bù hǎo*	My cooking is not good.
你还要...吗?	*nǐ hái yào...ma*	Would you like to have some more...
啤酒	*píjiǔ*	beer
米饭	*mǐfàn*	rice
汤	*tāng*	soup
随便吃。	*suíbiàn chī*	Please help yourself.
吃饱了吗?	*chī bǎo le ma*	Have you had enough?

menu reader

DRINKS

啤酒	*píjiǔ*	beer
不含酒精的	*bù hán jiǔjīng de*	alcohol-free
瓶装的	*píngzhuāng de*	bottled
黑啤	*hēipí*	dark
扎啤/鲜啤酒	*zhāpí/xiān píjiǔ*	draught
红茶	*hóng chá*	black tea
白兰地	*báilándì*	brandy
香槟	*xiāngbīn*	champagne
巧克力(热/冷)	*qiǎokèlì (rè/lěng)*	chocolate (hot/ cold)
鸡尾酒	*jīwěijiǔ*	cocktail
咖啡	*kāfēi*	coffee
清咖啡	*qīng kāfēi*	black
无咖啡因	*wú kāfēiyīn*	decaffeinated
冰	*bīng*	iced
牛奶咖啡	*niúnǎi kāfēi*	white
金酒及汤力水	*jīnjiǔ jí tānglìshuǐ*	gin and tonic
绿茶	*lǜ chá*	green tea
冰块儿	*bīngkuài'ér*	ice
冰茶	*bīng chá*	iced tea
茉莉花茶	*mòlìhuā chá*	jasmine tea
罐儿	*guànr*	jug
...汁	*...zhī*	...juice
苹果	*píngguǒ*	apple
柚子	*yòuzi*	grapefruit
橙子	*chéngzi*	orange
西红柿	*xīhóngshì*	tomato
柠檬汁	*níngméngzhī*	lemonade

奶昔	*nǎixī*	milkshake
牛奶(热/凉)	*niúnǎi (rè/liáng)*	milk (hot/cold)
矿泉水(带汽/不带汽)	*kuàngquán shuǐ (dàiqì/bú dàiqì)*	mineral water (fizzy/still)
红酒	*hóngjiǔ*	port
朗姆酒	*lǎngmǔjiǔ*	rum
苏打水	*sūdǎ shuǐ*	soda
奶茶	*nǎi chá*	tea with milk
伏特加	*fútèjiā*	vodka
葡萄酒	*pútáojiǔ*	wine
干	*gān*	dry
当地葡萄酒	*dāngdì pútáojiǔ*	local wine
红	*hóng*	red
玫瑰酒	*méiguījiǔ*	rosé
甜	*tián*	sweet
白	*bái*	white
威士忌	*wēishìjì*	whisky

RICE-BASED FOOD

白米饭	*bái mǐfàn*	boiled rice
蛋炒饭	*dàn chǎo fàn*	egg stir-fried rice
扬州炒饭	*yángzhōu chǎo fàn*	Yangzhou stir-fried rice
粽子	*zòngzi*	glutinous rice wrapped in bamboo leaves
锅巴饭	*guōbā fàn*	crispy rice topped with seafood, meat or vegetables
炒年糕	*chǎo nián gāo*	stir-fried New Year's rice cake

WHEAT-BASED FOOD

饼	*bǐng*	pancake
烧饼	*shāobǐng*	pancake with sesame seeds
葱油饼	*cōngyóu bǐng*	pancake with spring onion
馅儿饼	*xiànr bǐng*	pancake with fillings
包子	*bāozi*	filled steamed dumplings
猪肉包子	*zhūròu bāozi*	...with pork filling
牛肉包子	*niúròu bāozi*	...with beef filling
羊肉包子	*yángròu bāozi*	...with lamb filling
三鲜包子	*sān xiān bāozi*	...with 'three fresh' (usually meat with seafood)
素包子	*sù bāozi*	...with vegetables
豆沙包子	*dòu shā bāozi*	...with red-bean paste
小笼包子	*xiǎo lóng bāozi*	small steamed dumplings with fillings
面 /面条	*miàn/miàntiáo*	noodles
猪肉丝炒面	*zhū ròu sī chǎo miàn*	stir-fried noodles with shredded pork
豆芽炒面	*dòu yá chǎo miàn*	stir-fried noodles with bean-sprouts
炸酱面	*zhá jiàng miàn*	noodles with minced meat and soy bean
牛肉面	*niú ròu miàn*	noodles with beef
汤面	*tāng miàn*	noodles in soup

锅贴	*guō tiē*	fried dumplings
素饺子	*sù jiǎozi*	dumplings with vegetable fillings
馄饨	*hún tún*	won ton
春卷	*chūn juǎn*	spring rolls

CHINESE-STYLE BREAKFAST

馒头	*mántou*	steamed buns
花卷	*huā juǎn*	steamed twisted rolls
小笼包子	*xiǎo lóng bāozi*	small steamed dumplings with fillings
豆浆	*dòu jiāng*	soya milk
油条	*yóu tiáo*	deep-fried dough sticks
大米稀饭	*dàmǐ xīfàn*	rice porridge
松花蛋	*sōnghuā dàn*	preserved egg
咸鸭蛋	*xián yādàn*	salted duck egg
咸鸡蛋	*xián jīdàn*	salted chicken egg
咸菜	*xiáncài*	pickles

WESTERN-STYLE BREAKFAST

咸肉	*xiánròu*	bacon
香肠	*xiāngcháng*	sausage
煮鸡蛋	*zhǔ jīdàn*	boiled egg
煎鸡蛋	*jiān jīdàn*	fried egg
炒鸡蛋	*chǎo jīdàn*	scrambled eggs

面包	*miànbāo*	bread
烤面包	*kǎo miànbāo*	toast
黄油	*huángyóu*	butter
果酱	*guǒjiàng*	jam
酸奶	*suānnǎi*	yoghurt
糖	*táng*	sugar

SOUPS

鱼翅汤	*yú chì tāng*	shark's fin
三鲜汤	*sān xiān tāng*	'three fresh' (usually, meat, prawns and a vegetable)
海米紫菜汤	*hǎimǐ zǐcài tāng*	dried shrimp and seaweed
酸辣豆腐汤	*suān là dòufǔ tāng*	hot and sour tofu
菠菜粉丝汤	*bōcài fěnsī tāng*	spinach and vermicelli
什锦冬瓜汤	*shí jǐn dōngguā tāng*	winter marrow
西红柿鸡蛋汤	*xīhóngshì jīdàn tāng*	tomato and egg
时菜肉片汤	*shí cài ròu piàn tāng*	sliced pork and seasonal vegetable
冬菇肉片汤	*dōnggū ròu piàn tāng*	Chinese mushrooms with sliced pork

PORK, BEEF AND LAMB DISHES

猪肉	*zhūròu*	pork
粉蒸肉	*fěn zhēng ròu*	steamed pork with rice
红烧肉	*hóng shāo ròu*	pork belly braised in soy sauce
回锅肉	*huí guō ròu*	pork steamed and then stir-fried with chilli
狮子头	*shīzi tóu*	'lion's head' (minced pork balls)
蚂蚁上树	*mǎyi shàng shù*	'ants climbing the tree' (minced pork with vermicelli)
鱼香肉丝	*yú xiāng ròu sī*	stir-fried shredded pork with chilli, ginger and garlic
糖醋排骨	*táng cù páigǔ*	sweek and sour spareribs
木须肉	*mùxū ròu*	stir-fried sliced pork with eggs
叉烧肉	*chāshāo ròu*	barbecued pork
辣子肉丁	*làzi ròu dīng*	stir-fried diced pork with chilli
笋炒肉片	*sǔn chǎo ròu piàn*	stir-fried sliced pork with bamboo shoots
牛肉	*niúròu*	beef
五香干鞭牛肉丝	*wǔ xiāng gān biān niúròu sī*	deep-fried, shredded beef with five spices
卤/酱牛肉	*lǔ/jiàng niúròu*	pot-stewed beef in soy sauce

五香牛肉	*wǔ xiāng niúròu*	stewed beef with five spices
葱爆牛肉丝	*cōng bào niúròu sī*	shredded beef with spring onions
羊肉	*yángròu*	lamb/mutton
羊肉串	*yángròu chuàn*	lamb kebabs
涮羊肉	*shuàn yángròu*	Mongolian lamb hot pot
葱爆羊肉丝	*cōng bào yángròu sī*	shredded lamb with spring onions
羊肉泡馍	*yángròu pàomó*	braised lamb with pancake

CHICKEN AND DUCK DISHES

鸡	*jī*	chicken
香酥鸡	*xiāng sū jī*	crispy deep-fried chicken
白斩鸡	*bái zhǎn jī*	sliced cold chicken
宫保鸡丁	*gōng bǎo jī dīng*	stir-fried diced chicken with peanuts and chilli
叫花鸡	*jiàohuā jī*	'beggar's chicken' (charcoal-baked marinated chicken)
鸭/鸭子	*yā/yāzi*	duck
北京烤鸭	*běijīng kǎo yā*	Beijing roast duck
咸水鸭	*xián shuǐ yā*	steamed salted duck
香酥鸭	*xiāng sū yā*	crispy deep-fried duck

FISH AND SEAFOOD DISHES

鱼	*yú*	fish
滑溜鱼片	*huáliu yú piàn*	stir-fried fish slices with sauce
糖醋鱼块	*táng cù yú kuài*	sweet and sour fish
清蒸鲤鱼	*qîngzhēng lǐyú*	steamed carp
红烧鱼	*hóngshǎo yú*	fish braised in soy sauce
鱼头炖豆腐	*yú tóu dùn dòufu*	fish head stewed with tofu
芙蓉虾仁	*fúróng xiǎrén*	stir-fried shrimps with egg white
油焖大虾	*yóumèn dàxiǎ*	sauted king prawns
油焖龙虾	*yóumèn lóngxiǎ*	sauted lobsters
黄鳝	*huáng shàn*	paddyfield eel
炒鳝丝	*chǎo shàn sǐ*	stir-fried shredded paddyfield eel
清蒸螃蟹	*qǐngzhēng pángxiè*	steamed crab
炒鱿鱼	*chǎo yóuyú*	stir-fried squid
海参	*hǎi shēn*	sea cucumber
海蜇拌黄瓜	*hǎizhé bàn huángguǎ*	jellyfish with cucumber

VEGETABLES AND TOFU DISHES

蔬菜	*shūcài*	vegetable
炒豆芽	*chǎo dòu yá*	stir-fried bean sprouts
炒时菜	*chǎo shí cài*	stir-fried seasonal vegetables
冬笋炒扁豆	*dōng sǔn chǎo biǎn dòu*	stir-fried dwarf beans with bamboo shoots

鲜蘑炒豌豆	*xiān mó chǎo wāndòu*	stir-fried mushrooms with fresh peas
鱼香茄子	*yú xiāng qiézi*	aubergines with chilli, ginger and garlic
韭黄炒鸡蛋	*jiǔhuáng chǎo jīdàn*	stir-fried hotbed chives with egg
西红柿炒鸡蛋	*xīhóngshì chǎo jīdàn*	stir-fried tomato with egg
麻辣豆腐	*má là dòufu*	tofu with chilli and Sichuan pepper
沙锅炖豆腐	*shāguō dùn dòufu*	tofu braised in casserole
豆腐皮	*dòufu pí*	dried tofu sheets
五香豆腐干	*wǔ xiāng dòufu gān*	dried tofu with five spices
豆腐丝	*dòufu sī*	dried tofu shreds
素什锦	*sù shíjǐn*	assorted gluten with bamboo shoots

DESSERTS

八宝饭	*bā bǎo fàn*	'eight treasures' (rice pudding with nuts, dates, etc.)
元宵 /汤元	*yuánxiāo/tāngyuán*	sweet dumplings made with glutinous rice flour
拔丝苹果	*básī píngguǒ*	toffee apple
杏仁豆腐	*xìngrén dòufu*	almond tofu

sightseeing &activities

* at the travel agent

YOU MAY SEE...

关门	*guānmén*	closed
免费传单	*miǎnfèi chuándān*	free leaflets
饭店	*fàndiàn*	hotels
地图	*dìtú*	maps
开门	*kāimén*	open
票	*piào*	tickets
旅行社	*lǚxíng shè*	travel agency

YOU MAY WANT TO SAY...

Does someone speak English here?	这儿有人会说英文吗？	*zhèr yǒurén huì shuō yīnwén ma*
Do you have...	你有...吗？	*nǐ yǒu...ma*
a map of the town?	城市地图	*chéngshì dìtú*
Can you recommend a...	你能推荐一个...吗？	*nǐ néng tuījiàn yī ge...ma*
traditional restaurant?	传统饭店	*chuántǒng fàndiàn*
Do you have information...	你有... 的信息吗？	*nǐ yǒu... de xìnxí ma*
in English?	英文版	*yīngwén bǎn*
Can you book... for me?	你能给我定...吗？	*nǐ néng gěi wǒ dìng... ma*
this day trip	这个一日游	*zhège yī rì yóu*

Where is...	...在哪儿?	*...zài nǎr*
the museum?	博物馆	*bówùguǎn*
Can you show me on the map?	你能在地图上指给我看吗?	*nǐ néng zài dìtú shàng zhǐgěi wǒ kàn ma*

* opening times

(see **telling the time**, page 23)

YOU MAY WANT TO SAY...

What time does the museum open?	博物馆什么时候开门?	*bówùguǎn shénme shíhòu kāimén*
What time does the... close?	...几点关门?	*...jǐ diǎn guānmén*
archaeological site	考古工地	*kǎogǔ gōngdì*
When does the... open?	...几点开门?	*...jǐ diǎn kāimén*
exhibition	展览会	*zhǎnlǎnhuì*
Is it open...	...开门吗?	*...kāimén ma*
on Mondays?	星期一	*xīngqīyī*
at the weekend?	周末	*zhōumò*
Can we visit the...	我们可以参观...吗?	*wǒmen kěyǐ cānguān...ma*
temple?	寺庙	*sìmiào*
Is it open to the public?	这个对外开放吗?	*zhège duì wài kāifàng ma*

YOU MAY HEAR...

除了...每天都开门。	*chúle...měitiān dōu kāimén*	It's open every day except...
从...到...开门。	*cóng...dào...kāimén*	It's open from... to...
...关门。 星期日	*...guānmén* *xīngqīrì*	It's closed on... Sunday.
冬季关门。	*dōngjì guānmén*	It's closed in winter.
关门，正在修理。	*guānmén, zhèngzài xiūlǐ*	It's closed for repairs.

✻ visiting places

Please note that children's tickets are sold according to their height. Normally children under 1 metre 20 centimetres go free, and children above that height have to pay, but with a discount.

YOU MAY SEE...

关门(正在整修)。	*guānmén (zhèngzài zhěngxiū)*	closed (for restoration)
勿动。	*wù dòng*	do not touch
请勿入内/闲人免进。	*qǐng wù rùnèi/ xiánrén miǎnjìn*	no entry

请勿(用闪光灯)照相。	*qǐng wù (yòng shǎnguāngdēng) zhàoxiàng*	no (flash) photography
开门。	*kāimén*	open
售票处。	*shòupiào chǔ*	ticket office
厕所。	*cèsuǒ*	toilet

YOU MAY WANT TO SAY...

How much does it cost?	多少钱?	*duō shǎo qián*
One adult, please.	请给我一张成人票。	*qǐng gěi wǒ yī zhāng chéngrén piào*
A family ticket, please.	我要一张家庭票。	*wǒ yào yī zhāng jiātíng piào*
Is there a discount for...	...有折价吗?	*...yǒu zhéjià ma*
students?	学生	*xuéshēng*
senior citizens?	老人	*lǎo rén*
people with disabilities?	残疾人	*cánjí rén*
Is there...	有...吗?	*yǒu...ma*
wheelchair access?	坐轮椅的人的设施	*zuò lúnyǐ de rén de shèshī*
an audio tour?	语音讲解	*yǔyīn jiǎngjiě*
a picnic area?	野餐区	*yěcān qū*
Are there guided tours (in English)?	有(英文的)导游带队参观吗?	*yǒu (yīngwén de) dǎoyóu dài duì cānguān ma*

visiting places

Can I take photos?	我可以拍照吗？	*wǒ kěyǐ pāizhào ma*
Can you take a photo of us?	你能为我们拍张照片吗？	*nǐ néng wéi wǒmen pāi zhāng zhàopiàn ma*
When was this built?	这是什么时候造的？	*zhè shì shénme shíhòu zào de*
Who painted that?	那是谁画的？	*nà shì shéi huàde*
How old is it?	这有多少年头了？	*zhè yǒu duōshǎo niántóu le*

YOU MAY HEAR...

一个人五十元。	*yī ge rén wǔshí yuán*	It costs 50 yuan per person.
...有折扣。	*...yǒu zhékòu*	There's a discount for...
儿童	*értóng*	children
对不起，这儿不适合轮椅出入。	*duìbùqǐ, zhèr bú shìhé lúnyǐ chūrù*	I'm sorry, it's not suitable for wheelchairs.
你想加入一个有解说的观光团吗？	*nǐ xiǎng jiārù yī ge yǒu jiěshuō de guānguāngtuán ma*	Do you want to join a tour?
语音讲解三十元。	*yǔyīn jiǎngjiě sānshí yuán*	The audio tour costs 30 yuan.
这建造于...世纪。	*zhè jiànzào yú...shìjì*	It was built in the ... century.
这幅画画于...	*zhè fú huà huà yú*	It was painted in...
八十年代。	*bāshí niándài*	the eighties

* going on tours and trips

YOU MAY WANT TO SAY...

I'd like to join the tour to...	我想加入去...的旅游团。	*wǒ xiǎng jiārù qù... de lǚyóutuán*
What time does it...	什么时候...	*shénme shíhòu...*
leave?	离开?	*líkāi*
get back?	返回?	*fǎnhuí*
Where does it leave from?	从哪儿出发?	*cóng nǎr chūfā*
Does the guide speak English?	导游会说英文吗?	*dǎoyóu huì shuō yīngwén ma*
How much is it?	多少钱?	*duō shǎo qián*
Is...included?	包括...吗?	*bāokuò... ma*
lunch	午饭/中饭	*wǔfàn/zhōngfàn*
accommodation	住宿	*zhùsù*
When's the next...	下一趟...是什么时候?	*xià yī tàng...shì shénme shíhòu*
boat trip?	游船	*yóu chuan*
day trip?	当日游	*dāngrì yóu*
Can we hire...	我们能不能雇用一个...	*wǒmen néng bù néng gùyòng yī ge...*
an English-speaking guide?	会说英文的导游?	*huì shuō yīngwén de dǎoyóu*
I'm with a group.	我是跟团队一起来的。	*wǒ shì gēn tuánduì yīqǐ lái de*
I've lost my group.	我找不到我的团队了。	*wǒ zhǎo bù dào wǒde tuánduì le*

YOU MAY HEAR...

...点离开。	*...diǎn líkāi*	It leaves at...
...点返回。	*...diǎn fǎnhuí*	It gets back at...
从...发。	*cóng...chūfā*	It leaves from...
别迟到！	*bié chídào*	Don't be late!
他/她每天收费...元。	*tā/tā měitiān shōufèi...yuán*	He/She charges ... yuan per day.

* tourist glossary

YOU MAY SEE...

画廊/美术馆	*huà láng/měishù guǎn*	art gallery
墓地/公墓	*mùdì/gōngmù*	cemetery
教堂	*jiàotáng*	church
城墙	*chéng qiáng*	city wall
皇帝	*huángdì*	emperor
时代	*shídài*	era
展览	*zhǎnlǎn*	exhibition
堡垒	*bǎolěi*	fortress
花园	*huāyuán*	gardens
温泉	*wēn quán*	hot spring
寺庙	*sìmiào*	monastery
纪念碑	*jìniànbēi*	monument
博物馆	*bówùguǎn*	museum
画家	*huàjiā*	painter
宫殿	*gōngdiàn*	palace
公园	*gōngyuán*	park

名胜古迹	*míngshèng gǔjī*	places of historical interest
圣坛	*shèngtán*	shrine
纪念品	*jìniànpǐn*	souvenirs
体育馆	*tǐyùguǎn*	stadium
广场	*guǎngcháng*	square
庙/坛	*miào/tán*	temple
塔	*tǎ*	tower
动物园	*dòngwùyuán*	zoo

* entertainment

YOU MAY SEE...

后排	*hòu pái*	back row
芭蕾舞	*bālěiwǔ*	ballet
电影院	*diànyǐngyuàn*	cinema
杂技	*zájì*	circus
音乐大厅	*yīnyuè dàtīng*	concert hall
入口	*rùkǒu*	entrance
夜场	*yècháng*	evening performance
出口	*chūkǒu*	exit
前排	*qián pái*	front row
卡拉OK	*kǎlā OK*	karaoke
比赛	*bǐsài*	match
日场	*rìcháng*	matinée
夜总会	*yèzǒnghuì*	nightclub
歌剧院	*gējù yuàn*	opera house
交响乐	*jiāoxiǎngyuè*	orchestra
京剧	*jīng jù*	peking opera
赛马场	*sàimǎ cháng*	racecourse

排	*pái*	row
售完	*shòu wán*	sold out
话剧	*huà jù*	spoken play
剧院	*jùyuàn*	theatre
原文带字幕	*yuánwén dài zìmù*	original language version with subtitles
十八岁以上可以入内	*shíbā suì yǐshàng kěyǐ rùnèi*	over 18s only
没有幕间休息	*méi yǒu mùjiān xiūxí*	there is no interval
出售今日戏票	*chūshòu jīnrì xìpiào*	tickets for today's performance

YOU MAY WANT TO SAY...

What is there to do in the evenings here?	晚上有什么可以做的事情?	*wǎnshàng yǒu shénme kěyǐ zuò de shìqíng*
Is there anything for children?	有什么儿童活动吗?	*yǒu shénme értóng huódòng ma*
Is there... round here?	附近有...吗?	*fùjìn yǒu...ma*
a cinema	电影院	*diànyǐngyuàn*
What's on...	...上演什么?	*...shàngyǎn shénme*
tomorrow?	明天	*míngtiān*
at the theatre?	剧院	*jùyuàn*
When does the... start?	...什么时候开始?	*...shénme shíhòu kāishǐ*
performance	演出	*yǎnchū*
What time does it finish?	几点结束?	*jǐ diǎn jiéshù*

Where can I get tickets?	从哪儿能买到票?	*cóng nǎr néng mǎi dào piào*
Is it suitable for children?	适合孩子看吗?	*shìhé háizi kàn ma*
Has the film got subtitles?	电影有字幕吗?	*diànyǐng yǒu zìmù ma*
Is it dubbed?	是配音的吗?	*shì pèiyīn de ma*

YOU MAY HEAR...

...点开始?	*...diǎn kāishǐ*	It starts at...
...点结束?	*...diǎn jiéshù*	It finishes at...
大约... 两个小时。	*dàyuē...* *liǎng ge xiǎoshí*	It lasts about... two hours
有配音。	*yǒu pèiyīn*	It's dubbed.
有英文字幕。	*yǒu yīngwén zìmù*	It's got English subtitles.
你可以在这儿买票。	*nǐ kěyǐ zài zhèr mǎi piào*	You can buy tickets here.

✱ booking tickets

YOU MAY WANT TO SAY...

Can you get me tickets for... the ballet?	你能给我买到...的票吗? 芭蕾	*nǐ néng gěi wǒ mǎi dào... de piào ma* *bālěi*

Are there any seats left for Saturday?	星期六还有座位吗?	*xīngqīliù hái yǒu zuòwèi ma*
I'd like to book…	我想订…	*wǒ xiǎng ding…*
two seats	两个座位	*liǎng ge zuòwèi*
in the front row	要前排	*yào qián pái*
Do you have anything cheaper?	你有便宜些的票吗?	*nǐ yǒu piányí xiē de piào ma*

YOU MAY HEAR...

要多少张?	*yào duōshǎo zhāng*	How many?
要什么时候的?	*yào shénme shíhòu de*	When for?
我们不收信用卡。	*wǒmen bù shōu xìnyòng kǎ*	We don't accept credit cards.
对不起, 那天/那天晚上的卖完了。	*duìbùqǐ, nà tiān/nà tiān wǎnshàng de mài wán le*	I'm sorry we're sold out that day/night.

✻ at the show

YOU MAY WANT TO SAY...

Two for tonight's performance, please.	要两张今晚的票。	*yào liǎng zhāng jīnwǎn de piào*
How much is that?	多少钱?	*duō shǎo qián*

We'd like to sit...	我们想坐在...	*wǒmen xiǎng zuò zài...*
at the front	前排。	*qián pái*
at the back	后排。	*hòu pái*
in the middle	中间。	*zhōngjiān*
We've reserved seats.	我们预订了座位。	*wǒmen yùdìng le zuòwèi*
Is there an interval?	有幕间休息吗?	*yǒu mùjiān xiūxí ma*
Where are the toilets?	厕所在哪儿?	*cèsuǒ zài nǎr*
Can you stop talking, please?!	请你别说话，行吗?	*qǐng nǐ bié shuōhuà, xíng ma*

YOU MAY HEAR...

我能看一下你的信用卡吗?	*wǒ néng kàn yīxià nǐde xìnyòng kǎ ma*	Can I see your credit card, please?
对不起，我们全满了。	*duìbùqǐ, wǒmen quánmǎn le*	Sorry, we're full tonight.
你想坐在哪儿?	*nǐ xiǎng zuò zài nǎr*	Where do you want to sit?
你想要节目单吗?	*nǐ xiǎng yào jiémù dān ma*	Would you like a programme?

* sports and activities

Please note that in most indoor pools, ladies are required to wear swimming caps.

YOU MAY SEE...

海滩	*hǎitān*	beach
租船	*zū chuán*	boat hire
电缆车	*diànlǎn chē*	cable car
危险	*wéixiǎn*	danger
急救	*jí jiù*	first aid
足球场	*zúqiú chǎng*	football pitch
高尔夫球场	*gāo'ěrfū qiúchǎng*	golf course
健身房	*jiànshēnfáng*	gymnasium
骑马	*qí mǎ*	horse riding
武术	*wǔ shù*	martial art
不许钓鱼	*bùxǔ diàoyú*	no fishing
不许游泳	*bùxǔ yóuyǒng*	no swimming
私人住宅	*sīrén zhùzhái*	private property
租用滑雪用品	*zūyòng huáxuě yòngpǐn*	ski hire
滑雪学校	*huáxuě xuéxiào*	ski school
滑雪斜坡	*huáxuě xiépō*	ski slope
运动中心	*yùndòng zhōngxīn*	sports centre
游泳池（室内）	*yóuyǒng chí(shìnèi)*	swimming pool (indoor)
游泳池（室外）	*yóuyǒng chí(shìwài)*	swimming pool (outdoor)
乒乓球	*pīngpāng qiú*	table tennis
太极拳	*tàijí quán*	tai-chi
网球场	*wǎngqiú chǎng*	tennis court

YOU MAY WANT TO SAY...

Where can I/we...	我/我们可以在哪儿...	*wǒ/wǒmen kěyǐ zài nǎr...*
play tennis?	打网球?	*dǎ wǎngqiú*
play golf?	打高尔夫球?	*dǎ gāo'ěrfū qiú*
Can I/we...	我/我们能...吗?	*wǒ/wǒmen néng... ma*
go skiing?	滑雪	*huáxuě*
go swimming?	游泳	*yóuyǒng*
I'm...	我是...	*wǒ shì...*
a beginner	初学者	*chūxuézhě*
quite experienced	老手	*lǎo shǒu*
How much does it cost...	...多少钱?	*...duō shǎo qián*
per hour?	一个小时	*yīge xiǎoshí*
per day?	一天	*yī tiān*
per round?	一轮	*yī lún*
per game?	一局	*yī jú*
Can I/we hire...	我/我们能租...吗?	*wǒ/wǒmen néng zū... ma*
clubs?	高尔夫球杆	*gāo'ěrfū qiúgǎn*
racquets?	球拍	*qiúpāi*
Do you give lessons?	有培训课吗?	*yǒu péixùn kè ma*
Is there a discount for children?	儿童打折吗?	*értóng dǎzhé ma*
Where are the changing rooms?	更衣室在哪儿?	*gèngyī shì zài nǎr*

What's...	...怎么样?	*...zěnme yàng*
the water like?	水的状况	*shuǐ de zhuàngkuàng*
the snow like?	雪的状况	*xuě de zhuàngkuàng*

YOU MAY HEAR...

你是初学者吗?	*nǐ shì chūxuézhě ma*	Are you a beginner?
你会...吗?	*nǐ huì... ma*	Can you...
滑雪	*huáxuě*	ski?
风帆冲浪	*fēngfān chōnglàng*	windsurf?
每小时...元。	*měi xiǎoshí... yuán*	It costs... yuan per hour.
要交...元押金，是可以退还的。	*yào jiāo... yuán yājīn, shì kěyǐ tuìhuán de*	There's a refundable deposit of... yuan.
我们满员了。	*wǒmen mǎnyuán le*	We're fully booked.
稍后再来。	*shāo hòu zài lái*	Come back later.
明天有空位。	*míngtiān yǒu kōngwèi*	We've got places tomorrow.
你穿几号?	*nǐ chuān jǐ hào*	What size are you?
你需要...	*nǐ xūyào...*	You need...
一张照片。	*yī zhāng zhàopiān*	a photo
戴游泳帽。	*dài yóuyǒng mào*	to wear a swimming cap

shops&services

* shopping

- Prices are fixed in department stores and supermarkets, but in private-owned shops and markets one is expected to bargain.
- It would be extremely difficult to get a refund in most shops, so make sure that what you buy is to your satisfaction.

For Chinese currency terms, see **changing money**, page 141.

YOU MAY SEE...

古董店	*gǔdǒng diàn*	antiques
工艺美术	*gōngyì měishù*	art and craft stores
面包房	*miànbāo fáng*	bakery
书店	*shūdiàn*	bookshop
肉店	*ròudiàn*	butcher's
糕饼店	*gāobǐng diàn*	cake shop
收银台/收款	*shōuyín tái/shōukuǎn*	cashier
试衣室	*shìyī shì*	changing rooms
儿童用品	*értóng yòngpǐn*	children's
中药店	*zhōng yào diàn*	Chinese medicine shop
关门	*guānmén*	closed
服装	*fúzhuāng*	clothing
电脑	*diànnǎo*	computers
点心店	*diǎnxīn diàn*	confectioner's
化妆品	*huàzhuāngpǐn*	cosmetics
百货商店	*bǎihuò shāngdiàn*	department store
勿动	*wù dòng*	do not touch
干洗店	*gānxǐ diàn*	dry-cleaners

电器	*diànqì*	electrical goods
礼品	*lǐpǐn*	gifts
金店/金银店	*jīn diàn/jīnyín diàn*	gold shop
食品店	*shípǐn diàn*	groceries
美容/美发	*měiróng/měifā*	hairdresser's
健康食品	*jiànkāng shípǐn*	health foods
珠宝店	*zhūbǎo diàn*	jeweller's
皮革制品	*pígé zhìpǐn*	leather goods
电梯	*diàntī*	lifts
男厕所	*nán cèsuǒ*	men's
（全天）开门	*(quán tiān) kāimén*	open (all day)
眼镜店	*yǎnjìng diàn*	optician's
摄像/摄影	*shèxiàng/shèyǐng*	photographer's
丝绸店	*sīchóu diàn*	silk shop
鞋店	*xié diàn*	shoe shop
商业中心	*shāngyè zhōngxīn*	shopping centre
纪念品	*jìniànpǐn*	souvenirs
特价	*tè jià*	special offers
体育用品	*tǐyù yòngpǐn*	sports goods
文具店	*wénjù diàn*	stationer's
超市	*chāoshì*	supermarket
糖果店	*tángguǒ diàn*	sweet shop
裁缝店	*cáiféng diàn*	tailor's
烟酒店	*yān jiǔ diàn*	tobacco and alcohol
玩具店	*wánjù diàn*	toy shop
女厕所	*nǚ cèsuǒ*	women's

shopping

YOU MAY WANT TO SAY...

Where is...	...在哪儿?	*...zài nǎr*
the shopping centre?	商业中心	*shāngyè zhōngxīn*
the post office?	邮局	*yóu jú*
Where can I buy...	我在哪儿能买到...?	*wǒ zài nǎr néng mǎidào...*
suntan lotion?	防晒油	*fángshài yóu*
a map?	一张地图	*yī zhāng dìtú*
I'd like ..., please.	我想要...。	*wǒ xiǎng yào...*
that one there	那边的那个	*nàbiān de nàge*
this one here	这边的这个	*zhèbiān de zhège*
two of those	两个这个	*liǎng ge zhège*
Have you got...?	你有没有...?	*nǐ yǒu méi yǒu...*
How much is it?	多少钱?	*duō shǎo qián*
Can you write it down please?	你能写下来吗?	*nǐ néng xiě xiàlái ma*
I'm just looking.	我只是看看。	*wǒ zhǐshì kànkan*
I'll take it.	我要了。	*wǒ yào le*
Can you...	你能不能...?	*nǐ néng bù néng...*
keep it for me?	给我留下	*gěi wǒ liúxià*
order it for me?	给我订这个货	*gěi wǒ dìng zhège huò*
I need to think about it.	我需要想想。	*wǒ xūyào xiǎngxiang*

YOU MAY HEAR...

您想买什么?	*nín xiǎng mǎi shénme*	What would you like to buy?
五十块。	*wǔshí kuài*	It costs 50 yuan.
对不起，卖光了。	*duìbùqǐ, mài guāng le*	I'm sorry, we've sold out.
我们可以给您订。	*wǒmen kěyǐ gěi nín dìng*	We can order it for you.
我们明天有送货。	*wǒmen míngtiān yǒu sònghuò*	We'll have the delivery tomorrow.

* paying

YOU MAY WANT TO SAY...

Where do I pay?	我在哪儿付钱?	*wǒ zài nǎr fùqián*
Do you take credit cards?	你们收信用卡吗?	*nǐmen shōu xìnyòng kǎ ma*
Can you wrap it, please?	你能给我包起来吗?	*nǐ néng gěi wǒ bāo qǐlái ma*
Can I have... please?	可以给我...吗?	*kěyǐ gěi wǒ... ma*
a receipt	一张收据	*yī zhāng shōujù*
a bag	一个袋子	*yī ge dàizi*
Sorry, I haven't got any change.	对不起，我没有零钱。	*duìbùqǐ, wǒ méi yǒu língqián*

buying clothes and shoes

YOU MAY HEAR...

这是当礼品吗?	*zhè shì dāng lǐpǐn ma*	Is it a gift?
您想要包起来吗?	*nín xiǎng yào bāo qǐlái ma*	Do you want it wrapped?
您要袋子吗?	*nín yào dàizi ma*	Do you want a bag?
您如何付款?	*nín rúhé fùkuǎn*	How do you want to pay?
我能看一下... 吗?	*wǒ néng kàn yīxià... ma*	Can I see... please?
身份证明	*shēnfèn zhèngmíng*	some ID
护照	*hùzhào*	your passport
您有零钱吗?	*nín yǒu língqián ma*	Have you got any change?

✻ buying clothes and shoes

(see **clothes and shoe sizes**, page 27)

YOU MAY WANT TO SAY...

Have you got...	你们有... 吗?	*nǐmen yǒu...ma*
a smaller size?	小号的	*xiǎo hào de*
a larger size?	大号的	*dà hào de*
other colours?	其他颜色的	*qítā yánsè de*
I'm a size...	我穿...号	*wǒ chuān...hào*
I'm looking for...	我在找...	*wǒ zài zhǎo...*
a shirt	一件衬衫	*yī jiàn chènshān*
trousers	裤子	*kùzi*

A pair of…	一双…	*yī shuāng…*
sandals	凉鞋	*liángxié*
boots	靴子	*xuēzi*
Where are the changing rooms?	试衣室在哪儿?	*shìyī shì zài nǎr*

* changing rooms

YOU MAY WANT TO SAY…

Can I try this on, please?	我能试试这个吗?	*wǒ néng shìshi zhège ma*
It doesn't fit.	大小不合适。	*dà xiǎo bù héshì*
It's too…	太…了。	*tài…le*
big.	大	*dà*
small.	小	*xiǎo*
It doesn't suit me.	不适合我穿。	*bú shìhé wǒ chuān*

* bargaining

YOU MAY WANT TO SAY…

Is this your best price?	这是你最好的价吗?	*zhè shì nǐ zuìhǎo de jià ma*
It's too expensive.	太贵了。	*tài guì le*
Is there a discount for cash?	付现金打折吗?	*fù xiànjīn dǎzhé ma*
I'll give you…	我付你…	*wǒ fù nǐ…*
That's my final offer.	这是我最后的价格。	*zhè shì wǒ zuìhòu de jiàgé*

✻ cosmetics and toiletries

- Chemists' and drugstores only sell medicine and medical related products (see **at the chemist's**, page 150). If you want to buy cosmetics or toiletries, you need to go to a department store or supermarket.

YOU MAY WANT TO SAY...

I need...	我需要...	*wǒ xūyào...*
deodorant	腋下喷剂	*yèxià pēnjì*
sanitary towels	卫生巾	*wèishēng jīn*
shampoo	洗发液	*xǐfǎyè*
shower gel	洗澡液	*xǐzǎo yè*
tampons	月经棉塞	*yuèjīng miánsāi*
toothpaste	牙膏	*yágāo*
I am looking for...	我在找...	*wǒ zài zhǎo...*
a perfume	一种香水	*yī zhǒng xiāngshuǐ*
a (pink) nail varnish	一种(粉色)指甲油	*yī zhǒng(fěnsè) zhǐjia yóu*
I'd like some...	我想买一些...	*wǒ xiǎng mǎi yīxiē...*
make-up remover	去化妆霜	*qù huàzhuāng shuāng*

* photography

YOU MAY WANT TO SAY...

Can you print photos from a memory card?	能从记忆卡上印相片吗?	*néng cóng jìyì kǎ shàng yìn xiàngpiàn ma*
When will it/they be ready?	什么时候能好?	*shénme shíhòu néng hǎo*
Do you have an express service?	你们有加快冲洗吗?	*nǐmen yǒu jiākuài chōngxǐ ma*
Does it cost extra?	要多付钱吗?	*yào duō fù qián ma*
How much does it cost...	...多少钱?	*...duō shǎo qián*
per print?	印一张	*yìn yī zhāng*
I'd like...please	我想要...	*wǒ xiǎng yào...*
an 8MB memory card	一个8MB的记忆卡。	*yī ge bā MB de jìyì kǎ*
a disposable camera	一次性的照相机。	*yīcìxìng de zhàoxiàngjī*
My camera is broken.	我的照相机坏了。	*wǒde zhàoxiàngjī huài le*
Do you do repairs?	你们能修吗?	*nǐmen néng xiū ma*

YOU MAY HEAR...

要冲印多大的?	*yào chōngyìn duō dà de*	What size do you want your prints?
要光面还是绒面?	*yào guāngmiàn háishì róngmiàn*	Do you want them matt or gloss?

…取。	…qǔ	Come back…
明天	míngtiān	tomorrow.
一个小时后	yī ge xiǎoshí hòu	in an hour.
您要多少储存量的记忆卡?	nín yào duō shǎo chúcúnliàng de jìyì kǎ	What size memory card do you want?

* tobacco and alcohol

- Tobacco and alcoholic drinks are normally sold in the same shop.

YOU MAY WANT TO SAY...

Can I have a packet of…, please?	请给我一包…	qǐng gěi wǒ yī bāo…
Do you sell…	你们有…吗?	nǐ men yǒu…ma
lighters?	打火机	dǎhuǒjī
Do you sell loose tobacco?	你们有香烟丝吗?	nǐmen yǒu xiāngyānsī ma
Have you got any…	你们有… 吗?	nǐmen yǒu...ma
local wine?	当地产的葡萄酒	dāngdì chǎn de pútáojiǔ
imported beer?	进口啤酒	jìnkǒu píjiǔ
Is this sweet or dry?	这是甜的还是酸的?	zhè shì tiánde háishì suānde
I'll take...please.	我要…	wǒ yào…
a bottle	一瓶。	yī píng
a box	一箱。	yī xiāng

* at the post office

YOU MAY WANT TO SAY...

A stamp for... please.	请给我一张寄...的邮票。	*qǐng gěi wǒ yī zhāng jì... de yóupiào*
Europe	欧洲	*ōuzhōu*
America	美国	*měiguó*
Australia	澳大利亚	*àodàlìyà*
Five stamps please.	要五张邮票。	*yào wǔ zhāng yóupiào*
For...	是寄...	*shì jì...*
postcards	明信片。	*míngxìnpiàn*
letters	信件。	*xìnjiàn*
Can I send this...	我能寄...吗?	*wǒ néng jì...ma*
registered?	挂号	*guàhào*
by airmail?	航空	*hángkōng*
by seamail?	海运	*hǎiyùn*
It contains...	里面有...	*lǐmiàn yǒu...*
a present.	一件礼物。	*yī jiàn lǐwù*
something valuable.	贵重东西。	*guìzhòng dōngxī*
something fragile.	容易打破的东西。	*róngyì dǎpò de dōngxī*
Can I have a receipt, please?	我能要一张收据吗?	*wǒ néng yào yī zhāng shōujù ma*

YOU MAY HEAR...

这是寄到哪儿的?	*zhè shì jì dào nǎr de*	Where is it going to?
明信片还是信?	*míngxìnpiàn háishì xìn*	For postcards or letters?
请放在秤上。	*qǐng fàng zài chèng shàng*	Put it on the scales, please.
里面有什么?	*lǐmiàn yǒu shénme*	What's in it?
请填写海关申报单。	*qǐng tiánxiě hǎiguān shēnbào dān*	Please fill in this customs declaration form.

✱ at the bank

YOU MAY WANT TO SAY...

Excuse me, where's the foreign exchange counter?	对不起, 兑换外币的柜台在哪儿?	*duìbùqǐ, duìhuàn wàibì de guìtái zài nǎr*
Is there a cashpoint machine here?	这儿有现钞机吗?	*zhèr yǒu xiànchāo jī ma*
The cashpoint machine has eaten my card.	现钞机吃进了我的卡。	*xiànchāo jī chī jìn le wǒde kǎ*
I've forgotten my pin number.	我忘了我的密码。	*wǒ wàng le wǒde mìmǎ*
Can I check my account, please?	我能查一下我的账吗?	*wǒ néng chá yīxià wǒde zhàng ma*

My account number is...	我的账号是...	*wǒde zhàng hào shì...*
My name is...	我的名字是...	*wǒde míngzì shì...*
I'd like to... withdraw some money	我想... 取一些钱。	*wǒ xiǎng... qǔ yīxiē qián*
Has my money arrived yet?	我的钱到了吗?	*wǒde qián dào le ma*

YOU MAY HEAR...

请出示证件。	*qǐng chūshì zhèngjiàn*	Your ID, please.
请给我你的护照。	*qǐng gěi wǒ nǐde hùzhào*	Your passport, please.
你叫什么?	*nǐ jiào shénme*	What's your name?
我们不能再多给你钱了。	*wǒmen bù néng zài duō gěi nǐ qián le*	We can't let you have any more money.

* changing money

- You can exchange foreign currency or traveller's cheques in major banks or at foreign exchange counters in large hotels. China is still mainly a cash-carrying society.

changing money

- The formal name for Chinese currency is 人民币 (*rénmín bì*) and it is abbreviated as RMB with the sign ¥. In Chinese currency, there are three units: 元 (*yuán*), 角 (*jiǎo*) and 分 (*fēn*). The informal terms are 块 (*kuài*), 毛 (*máo*) and 分 (*fēn*). Each unit contains 10 units of the next level down. So, if you see this price ¥1.54, it is read 一元五角四分 (*yī yuán wǔ jiǎo sì fēn*) or 一块五毛四分 (*yī kuài wǔ máo sì fēn*).

YOU MAY WANT TO SAY...

I'd like to change ..., please.	我想换...	*wǒ xiǎng huàn...*
these travellers' cheques	这些旅行支票。	*zhèxiē lǚxíng zhīpiào*
one hundred pounds	一百英镑。	*yī bǎi yīngbàng*
Can I have some change?	可以给我一些零钱吗?	*kěyǐ gěi wǒ yīxiē língqián ma*
Can I get money out on my credit card?	我能用信用卡取钱吗?	*wǒ néng yòng xìnyòng kǎ qǔ qián ma*
What's the rate today...	今天的... 汇率是多少?	*jīntiān de... huìlǜ shì duō shǎo*
for the pound?	英镑	*yīngbàng*
for the dollar?	美元	*měiyuán*
for the euro?	欧元	*ōuyuán*

YOU MAY HEAR...

换多少?	*huàn duō shǎo*	How much?
请出示护照。	*qǐng chūshì hùzhào*	Passport, please.
请在这儿签名。	*qǐng zài zhèr qiānmíng*	Sign here, please.
一英镑对十五块人民币。	*yī yīngbàng duì shíwǔ kuài rénmínbì*	It's 15 yuan to the pound.

* telephones

● Note that some phone cards can only be used in the city you are in, but others can be used nationally. Public phones which allow you to dial international numbers direct can only be found in large cities. They display the sign IDD (international direct dialling). There are many public phone booths which are attended by assistants. You can also make international calls from main post offices and post and telecommunications offices.

YOU MAY SEE...

公用电话	*gōngyòng diànhuà*	public phone
电话亭	*diànhuà tíng*	telephone booth
邮电局	*yóudiàn jú*	post and telecommunications office
邮局	*yóu jú*	post office
电报电话	*diànbào diànhuà*	telegrams and telephones

国内直拨	guónèi zhí bō	national direct dialling
国际直拨	guójì zhí bō	international direct dialling
手机	shǒujī	mobile
出售充值卡，SIM卡	chūshòu chōng zhí kǎ,SIM kǎ	pay-as-you-go card, SIM card for sale
网吧	wǎngbā	internet bar/café

YOU MAY WANT TO SAY...

Where's the (nearest) phone?	离这儿最近的电话在哪儿?	lí zhèr zuìjìn de diànhuà zài nǎr
Is there a public phone?	有公用电话吗?	yǒu gōngyòng diànhuà ma
Can I have some change for the phone, please?	我可以换一些零钱打电话吗?	wǒ kěyǐ huàn yīxiē língqián dǎ diànhuà ma
I'd like to...	我想...	wǒ xiǎng...
buy a phone card.	买一张电话卡。	mǎi yī zhāng diànhuà kǎ
call England.	打电话到英国。	dǎ diànhuà dào yīngguó
make a reverse charge call.	打个对方付款电话。	dǎ ge duìfāng fùkuǎn diànhuà
The number is...	号码是...	hàomǎ shì...
Can I use this card in other cities?	这个卡能在其他城市用吗?	zhè ge kǎ néng zài qítā chéngshì yòng ma

How much does it cost per minute?	每分钟多少钱?	*měi fēnzhōng duō shǎo qián*
What's the area code for...?	...的区号是什么?	*...de qūhào shì shénme*
What's the country code?	国家号是什么?	*guójiā hào shì shénme*
How do I get an outside line?	打外线怎么打?	*dǎ wàixiàn zěnme dǎ*
Hello.	喂	*wèi*
It's ... speaking.	是...	*shì...*
Can I have extension... please?	请接...分机	*qǐng jiē... fēnjī*
Can I speak to...?	我找...	*wǒ zhǎo...*
When will he/she be back?	他/她什么时候回来?	*tā/ tā shénme shíhòu huílái*
I'll ring back.	我一会儿再打回来。	*wǒ yīhuìr zài dǎ huílái*
Can I leave a message?	我能留个口信吗?	*wǒ néng liú ge kǒuxìn ma*
Can you tell him/ her ... called?	你能告诉他/她... 来电话了吗?	*nǐ néng gàosù tā/ tā... lái diànhuà le ma*
My number is...	我的号码是...	*wǒde hàomǎ shì...*
Sorry, I've got the wrong number.	对不起，我打错号码了。	*duìbùqǐ, wǒ dǎ cuò hàomǎ le*
It's a bad line.	线路不清。	*xiànlù bù qīng*
I've been cut off.	刚才线断了。	*gāngcái xiàn duàn le*

mobiles

YOU MAY HEAR...

喂。	*wèi*	Hello.
你找谁?	*nǐ zhǎo shéi*	Who's calling?
对不起,他/她不在。	*duìbùqǐ, tā/ tā bù zài*	Sorry,he/she's not here.
请稍等。	*qǐng shāo děng*	Just a moment.
占线。	*zhànxiàn*	It's engaged.
没人接。	*méi rén jiē*	There's no answer.
你要等吗?	*nǐ yào děng ma*	Do you want to hold?
对不起，号码不对。	*duìbùqǐ, hàomǎ bú duì*	Sorry, wrong number.

✻ mobiles

- Mobile phones are very popular in China. If you take your mobile phone with you, you can buy a pay-as-you go SIM card. There is a two-way charge for making and receiving calls.

YOU MAY WANT TO SAY...

Have you got...	你们有...吗?	*nǐmen yǒu...ma*
a charger for this phone?	这种电话的充电器	*zhè zhǒng diànhuà de chōngdiànqì*
a pay-as-you-go card?	充值卡	*chōngzhí kǎ*
Can I/we hire a mobile?	我/我们可以租个手机吗?	*wǒ/ wǒmen kěyǐ zū ge shǒujī ma*

What's the tariff?	是什么价?	*shì shénme jià*
Are text messages included?	包括短信吗?	*bāokuò duǎnxìn ma*
How do you make a local call?	怎么打当地电话?	*zěnme dǎ dāngdì diànhuà*
Is there a code?	有什么密码吗?	*yǒu shénme mìmǎ ma*

* the internet

YOU MAY SEE...

用户名	*yònghùmíng*	username
密码	*mìmǎ*	password
点击此处	*diǎnjí cǐchǔ*	click here
链接	*liánjiē chǔ*	link

YOU MAY WANT TO SAY...

Is there an internet café near here?	附近有网吧吗?	*fùjìn yǒu wǎngbā ma*
I'd like to check my emails.	我想查我的电子邮件。	*wǒ xiǎng chá wǒde diànzi yóujiàn*
How much is it per minute?	每分钟多少钱?	*měi fēnzhōng duō shǎo qián*
I can't log on.	我登不了陆。	*wǒ dēng bù liǎo lù*
It's not connecting.	接不上。	*jiē bú shàng*

It's very slow.	太慢了。	*tài màn le*
Can you...	你能把这个... 吗?	*nǐ néng bǎ zhège... ma*
print this?	印出来	*yìn chūlai*
scan this?	扫描	*sǎomiáo*
Can I...	我能...吗?	*wǒ néng...ma*
download this?	下载这个	*xiàzài zhège*
use my memory stick?	用我的记忆棒	*yòng wǒde jìyì bàng*
Do you have...	你有... 吗?	*nǐ yǒu...ma*
a CD-Rom?	多媒体光盘	*duō méitǐ guāngpán*

* faxes

YOU MAY WANT TO SAY...

What's your fax number?	你的传真号是多少?	*nǐde chuánzhēn hào shì duō shǎo*
Can you send this fax for me, please?	你能给我发这个传真吗?	*nǐ néng gěi wǒ fā zhège chuánzhēn ma*
How much is it?	多少钱?	*duō shǎo qián*

health&safety

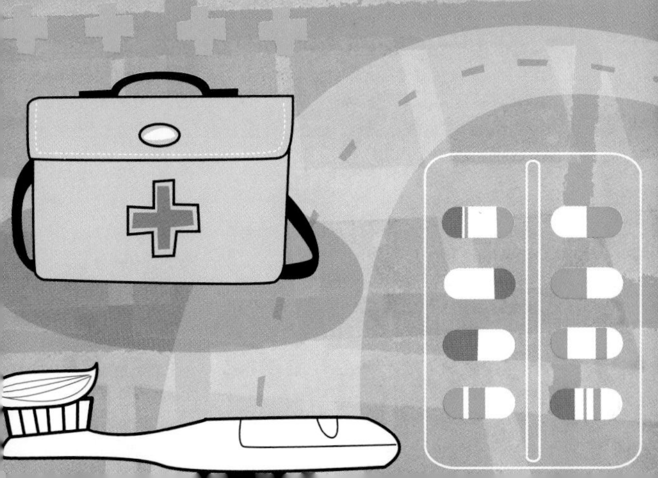

* at the chemist's

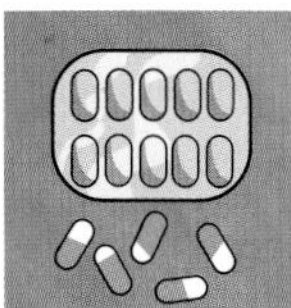

- Most chemists sell both western medicine and Chinese medicine, but some only sell Chinese medicine. For western medicine, only non-prescription medicines are sold at chemists. Prescribed medicines can only be obtained from the clinic or hospital in which the doctor you see works. For Chinese medicine, both prescription and non-prescription medicine are sold.

- Toiletries and cosmetics are normally sold in department stores and supermarkets.

YOU MAY SEE...

药店	*yàodiàn*	**chemist's/ drugstore**
中药	*zhōng yào*	**Chinese medicine**
西药	*xī yào*	**Western medicine**

YOU MAY WANT TO SAY...

Have you got something for...	你们有治...的药吗？	*nǐmen yǒu zhì... de yào ma*
diarrhoea?	拉肚子	*lādùzi*
headaches?	头疼	*tóu téng*
a sore throat?	嗓子疼	*sǎngzi téng*
Where can I buy suntan lotion?	我在哪儿能买到防晒霜？	*wǒ zài nǎr néng mǎidào fángshài shuāng*

I need some ... please.	我需要一些...	*wǒ xūyào yīxiē...*
condoms	避孕套。	*bìyùntào*
insect repellent	去蚊虫喷雾剂。	*qù wénchóng pēnwùjì*
painkillers	止痛药。	*zhǐtòng yào*
travel sickness pills	晕车药。	*yūnchē yào*

YOU MAY HEAR...

你吃过这种药吗?	*nǐ chīguò zhèzhǒng yào ma*	Have you taken this before?
你得去百货商店买那些。	*nǐ děi qù bǎihuò shāngdiàn mǎi nàxiē*	You have to buy them from a department store.
你得从医院的药房取这个药。	*nǐ děi cóng yīyuàn de yàofáng qǔ zhège yào*	You have to get it from the hospital's pharmacy.

✻ Chinese medicine

YOU MAY WANT TO SAY...

I'd like to try...	我想试试...	*wǒ xiǎng shìshi*
some herbal medicine	中草药。	*zhōng cǎoyào*
acupuncture	针灸。	*zhēnjiǔ*

Chinese medicine

Do you do traditional Chinese massage?	你们有中医按摩吗?	*nǐmen yǒu zhōngyī ànmó ma*
Can you make up this prescription, please?	请你给我配这个药方。	*qǐng nǐ gěi wǒ pèi zhège yàofāng*

YOU MAY HEAR...

我号一下你的脉,好吗?	*wǒ hào yīxià nǐde mài, hǎo ma*	May I feel your pulse?
请把舌头伸出来。	*qǐng bǎ shétóu shēn chūlái*	Can you stick your tongue out please?
你的胃口 怎么样?	*nǐde wèikǒu zěnme yàng*	How is your appetite?
你想要中成药还是干草药?	*nǐ xiǎng yào zhōng chéngyào háishì gàn cǎoyào*	Do you want to have ready-made herbal medicine or dried herbs?
你有处方吗?	*nǐ yǒu chǔfāng ma*	Have you got a prescription?

* at the doctor's

(see **medical complaints and conditions**, page 155)

YOU MAY WANT TO SAY...

I need a doctor (who speaks English).	我需要看医生(会说英文的)。	*wǒ xūyào kàn yīshēng(huì shuō yīngwén de)*
Can I make an appointment for...	我能约...看医生吗?	*wǒ néng yuē...kàn yīhēng ma*
today?	今天	*jīntiān*
tomorrow?	明天	*míngtiān*
I've run out of my medication.	我的药吃完了。	*wǒde yào chī wán le*
I'm on medication for...	我目前吃药治...	*wǒ mùqián chī yào zhì...*
I've had a ... jab.	我已经打过...的预防针了。	*wǒ yǐjīng dǎ guò... de yùfángzhēn le*
tetanus	破伤风	*pòshāngfēng*
He/She has had a ... vaccination.	他/她打过...的预防针。	*tā/tā dǎ guò...de yùfángzhēn*
polio	小儿麻痹症	*xiǎo'ér mábì zhèng*
measles	麻疹	*mázhěn*
Can I have a receipt for my health insurance, please?	请给我开一张收据,为了我的健康保险。	*qǐng gěi wǒ kāi yī zhāng shōujù, wéi le wǒde jiànkāng bǎoxiǎn*
I do not want an injection.	我不要打针。	*wǒ bú yào dǎzhēn*
Where do I get the medicine?	在哪儿取药?	*zài nǎr qǔ yào*

health and safety

✱ describing your symptoms

(for **parts of the body** see page 158)

YOU MAY WANT TO SAY...

• I don't feel well.	我不舒服。	*wǒ bù shūfu*
• It hurts here.	这儿疼。	*zhèr téng*
• My...hurts.	我的..疼。	*wǒde...téng*
stomach	肚子	*dùzi*
• I've got...	我...	*wǒ...*
a sore throat	嗓子疼。	*sǎngzi téng*
swollen glands	淋巴肿大。	*línbā zhǒngdà*
• I'm dizzy.	我头晕。	*wǒ tóuyūn*
• I feel sick.	我恶心。	*wǒ ěxīn*
• I can't ...	我...	*wǒ...*
breathe properly	喘不上气。	*chuǎn bù shàng qì*
sleep properly	睡不好觉。	*shuì bù hǎo jiào*
• My...is bleeding.	我的...流血了。	*wǒde...liúxiě le*
nose	鼻子	*bízi*
arm	胳膊	*gēbo*
• I've cut/burnt myself.	我弄破了/烧伤了自己。	*wǒ nòngpò le/ shāoshāng le zìjǐ*
• I've been sick.	我吐了。	*wǒ tù le*

* medical complaints and conditions

YOU MAY WANT TO SAY...

I'm...	我有...	*wǒ yǒu...*
arthritic	风湿。	*fēngshī*
asthmatic	哮喘。	*xiàochuǎn*
diabetic	糖尿病。	*tángniàobìng*
epileptic	羊角风。	*yángjiǎofēng*
I've got...	我有...	*wǒ yǒu...*
high/low blood pressure	高/低血压。	*gāo/dī xiěyā*
a heart condition	心脏病。	*xīnzàng bìng*
I'm...	我...	*wǒ...*
blind	是盲人。	*shì mángrén*
deaf	耳聋。	*ěrlóng*
pregnant	怀孕了。	*huáiyùn le*
I use a wheelchair.	我用轮椅。	*wǒ yòng lúnyǐ*
I have difficulty walking.	我走路有困难。	*wǒ zǒulù yǒu kùnnán*
I'm HIV positive.	我是艾滋病病毒携带者。	*wǒ shì àizībìng bìngdú xiédàizhě*
I don't want to have injections.	我不要打针。	*wǒ bú yào dǎzhēn*
I'm allergic to...	我对...过敏。	*wǒ duì... guòmǐn*
antibiotics	抗菌素	*kàngjùnsù*
cortisone	可的松	*kědìsōng*
nuts	果仁	*guǒrén*
penicillin	盘尼西林	*pánníxīlín*

YOU MAY HEAR...

什么地方疼?	*shénme dìfāng téng*	Where does it hurt?
这儿疼吗?	*zhèr téng ma*	Does it hurt here?
你从什么时候开始有这种感觉的?	*nǐ cóng shénme shíhòu kāishǐ yǒu zhè zhǒng gǎnjué de*	How long have you been feeling like this?
你在吃药吗?	*nǐ zài chī yào ma*	Are you on medication?
你是否患有	*nǐ shìfǒu huànyǒu...*	Have you got a history of...
肺炎?	*fèiyán*	chest infections?
你是否对什么过敏?	*nǐ shìfǒu duì shénme guòmǐn*	Are you allergic to anything?
你多大了?	*nǐ duō dà le*	How old are you?
请张开嘴。	*qǐng zhāngkāi zuǐ*	Open your mouth, please.
我需要量一下你的体温。	*wǒ xūyào liàng yīxià nǐde tǐwēn*	I need to take your temperature.
请脱衣服。	*qǐng tuō yīfú*	Get undressed, please.
请躺下。	*qǐng tǎngxià*	Lie down here, please.
不要紧。	*bú yàojǐn*	It's nothing serious.
你有炎症。	*nǐ yǒu yánzhèng*	You've got an infection.

你得化验。	*nǐ děi huàyàn…*	I need a … sample.
血	*xiě*	blood
尿	*niào*	urine
大便	*dàbiàn*	stool
你需要作X光。	*nǐ xūyào zuò X guāng*	You need an X-ray.
我得给你打针。	*wǒ děi gěi nǐ dǎzhēn*	I'm going to give you an injection.
一天两次，一次一片。	*yī tiān liǎng cì, yī cì yī piàn*	Take one tablet twice a day.
你必须休息。	*nǐ bìxū xiūxi*	You must rest.
你绝不能喝酒。	*nǐ jué bù néng hē jiǔ*	You mustn't drink alcohol.
你回国后一定要看医生。	*nǐ huí guó hòu yīdìng yào kàn yīshēng*	You should see a doctor when you go home.
你需要去医院。	*nǐ xūyào qù yīyuàn*	You need to go to hospital.
你扭伤了你的。	*nǐ niǔshāng le nǐde...*	You've sprained your...
踝关节	*huáiguānjié*	ankle
你的...骨折了。	*nǐde...gǔzhé le*	You've broken your...
胳膊	*gēbó*	arm
你得了	*nǐ dé le...*	You've got...
流感。	*liúgǎn*	flu
阑尾炎。	*lánwěiyán*	appendicitis
肺炎。	*fèiyán*	bronchitis

你...了。 食物中毒	*nǐ...le* *shíwù zhòngdú*	You've got... food poisoning
这是心脏病发作。	*zhè shì xīnzàngbìng fāzuò*	It's a heart attack.
你三天后必须再来。	*nǐ sān tiān hòu bìxū zài lái*	You must come back in three days' time.
你有处方吗？	*nǐ yǒu chǔfāng ma*	Have you got a prescription?

* parts of the body

YOU MAY WANT TO SAY...

ankle	踝关节	*huáiguānjié*
appendix	阑尾炎	*lánwěiyán*
arm	胳膊	*gēbó*
artery	动脉血管	*dòngmàixiěguǎn*
back	背	*bèi*
bladder	膀胱	*bǎngguāng*
blood	血	*xiě*
body	身子	*shēnzi*
bone	骨头	*gǔtóu*
bottom	屁股	*pìgǔ*
bowels	肠子	*chángzi*
breast	乳房	*rǔfáng*
chest	胸部	*xiōngbù*
collar bone	锁骨	*suǒgú*
ear	耳朵	*ěrduǒ*

elbow	肘部	*zhǒubù*
eye	眼睛	*yǎnjīng*
face	脸	*liǎn*
finger	手指	*shǒuzhǐ*
foot	脚	*jiǎo*
genitals	生殖器	*shēngzhíqì*
gland	腺状组织	*xiànzhuàngzǔzhī*
hand	手	*shǒu*
head	头	*tóu*
heart	心脏	*xīnzàng*
heel	脚后跟	*jiǎohòugēn*
hip	臀部	*túnbù*
jaw	下巴	*xiàbā*
joint	关节	*guānjié*
kidney	肾	*shèn*
knee	膝盖	*xīgài*
leg	腿	*tuǐ*
ligament	韧带	*rèndài*
liver	肝	*gān*
lung	肺部	*fèibù*
mouth	嘴	*zuǐ*
muscle	肌肉	*jīròu*
nail	指甲	*zhǐjia*
neck	脖子	*bózi*
nerve	神经	*shénjīng*
nose	鼻子	*bízi*
penis	阴茎	*yīnjīng*
rib	肋骨	*lèigǔ*
shoulder	肩膀	*jiānbǎng*
skin	皮肤	*pífū*
spine	脊椎	*jízhuī*

stomach	胃	*wèi*
tendon	腱	*jiàn*
testicle	睾丸	*gāowán*
thigh	大腿	*dàtuǐ*
throat	喉咙	*hóulóng*
thumb	手拇指	*shǒumǔzhǐ*
toe	脚指	*jiǎozhǐ*
tongue	舌头	*shétóu*
tonsils	扁桃体	*biǎntáotǐ*
tooth	牙齿	*yáchǐ*
vagina	阴道	*yīndào*
vein	静脉	*jìngmài*
wrist	手腕	*shǒuwàn*

* at the dentist's

YOU MAY WANT TO SAY...

I need a dentist (who speaks English).	我需要看牙医(会说英文的)。	*wǒ xūyào kàn yáyī (huì shuō yīngwén de)*
I've got toothache.	我牙疼。	*wǒ yáténg*
It (really) hurts.	(真的)特别疼。	*(zhēnde) tèbié téng*
It's my wisdom tooth.	是我的智齿。	*shì wǒde zhìchǐ*
I've lost ...	我的...掉了。	*wǒde...diào le*
a filling	补牙里的填料	*bǔyá lǐ de tiánliào*
a crown/cap	牙套	*yátào*

I've broken a tooth.	我磕坏了一个牙。	*wǒ kē huài le yī ge yá*
Can you fix it temporarily?	你能暂时弄好吗？	*nǐ néng zànshí nòng hǎo ma*

YOU MAY HEAR...

张大。	*zhāng dà*	Open wide.
将下巴合上。	*jiāng xiàbā héshàng*	Close your jaws together.
你需要照X光。	*nǐ xūyào zhào X guāng*	You need an x-ray.
你怀孕了吗？	*nǐ huáiyùn le ma*	Are you pregnant?
你的牙需要补。	*nǐde yá xūyào bǔ*	You need a filling.
我得拔这个牙	*wǒ děi bá zhège yá*	I'll have to take it out.
我要给你	*wǒ yào gěi nǐ...*	I'm going to give you...
打一针	*dǎ yī zhēn*	an injection
放临时填料	*fàng línshí tiánliào*	a temporary filling
装个临时的牙套	*zhuāng ge línshí de yátào*	a temporary crown

* emergencies

EMERGENCY TELEPHONE NUMBERS:

Police: **110**
Fire: **119**
Traffic accident: **112**
Ambulance: **120**
Beijing Red Cross First Aid Centre: **999**

YOU MAY SEE...

诊所	*zhēnsuǒ*	clinic
医生	*yīshēng*	doctor
急诊(部)	*jízhēn(bù)*	emergency (department)
急救	*jí jiù*	first aid
外用	*wài yòng*	for external use only
医院	*yīyuàn*	hospital
说明书	*shuōmíngshū*	instructions for use
护士	*hùshì*	nurse
有毒	*yǒudú*	poison
用前摇晃	*yòng qián yáohuǎng*	shake before use

YOU MAY WANT TO SAY...

I need...	我需要...	*wǒ xūyào...*
a doctor	一位医生	*yī wèi yīshēng*
an ambulance	一辆救护车	*yī liàng jiùhùchē*
the fire brigade	消防队	*xiāofángduì*
the police	警察	*jǐngchá*

Immediately!	十万火急！	*shíwànhuǒjí*
Help!	救命！	*jiùmìng*
Please help me/us.	请帮助我/我们。	*qǐng bāngzhù wǒ/ wǒmen*
There's a fire!	着火了。	*zháohuǒ le*
There's been an accident.	出事故了。	*chū shìgù le*
I have to use the phone.	我必须用一下电话。	*wǒ bìxū yòng yīxià diànhuà*
I'm lost.	我迷路了。	*wǒ mílù le*
I've lost my... son/daughter	我丢了我的... 儿子/女儿	*wǒ diū le wǒde... érzi/nǚ'ér*
Stop!	住手！	*zhùshǒu*

* police

YOU MAY WANT TO SAY...

Sorry, I didn't realise it was against the law.	对不起，我不知道这是违法的。	*duìbùqǐ, wǒ bù zhīdào zhè shì wéifǎ de*
Here are my documents.	这是我的证件。	*zhè shì wǒde zhèngjiàn*
I haven't got my passport on me.	我没带护照。	*wǒ méi dài hùzhào*
I don't understand.	我不明白。	*wǒ bù míngbái*
I'm innocent.	我是无辜的。	*wǒ shì wúgū de*

I need a lawyer (who speaks English).	我需要律师(会说英文的)。	*wǒ xūyào lǜshī(huì shuō yīngwén de)*
I want to contact my...	我要和我的...联系。	*wǒ yào hé wǒde... liánxì*
embassy	大使馆	*dàshǐguǎn*
consulate	领事馆	*lǐngshìguǎn*

YOU MAY HEAR...

你得付罚款。	*nǐ děi fù fákuǎn*	You'll have to pay a fine.
请出示你的证件。	*qǐng chūshì nǐde zhèngjiàn*	Your documents please.
你有什么可以证明你的身份吗?	*nǐ yǒu shénme kěyǐ zhèngmíng nǐde shēnfèn ma*	Have you got any proof of your identity?
跟我来。	*gēn wǒ lái*	Come with me.
你被捕了。	*nǐ bèibǔ le*	You're under arrest.

* reporting crime

YOU MAY WANT TO SAY...

I want to report a theft.	我想检举一个偷盗案。	*wǒ xiǎng jiǎnjǔ yī ge tōudào'àn*
I've been attacked.	我被人打了。	*wǒ bèi rén dǎ le*

My...has been stolen.	我的...被偷了。	*wǒde...bèi tōu le*
purse/wallet	钱包	*qiánbāo*
passport	护照	*hùzhào*
Our car has been broken into.	我们的车被撬开了。	*wǒmende chē bèi qiàokāi le*
I've lost my...	我丢了我的...	*wǒ diū le wǒde...*
credit cards	信用卡	*xìnyòng kǎ*
luggage	行李	*xínglǐ*
I've been mugged.	我被抢了。	*wǒ bèi qiǎng le*

YOU MAY HEAR...

是什么时候发生的?	*shì shénme shíhòu fāshēng de*	When did it happen?
在什么地方?	*zài shénme dìfāng*	Where?
是怎么回事?	*shì zěnme huí shì*	What happened?
他们长得什么样?	*tāmen zhǎngde shénme yàng*	What did they look like?

YOU MAY WANT TO SAY...

It happened...	发生在...	*fāshēng zài...*
five minutes ago	五分钟前	*wǔ fēnzhōng qián*
last night	昨晚	*zuó wǎn*

reporting crime

He/She had...	他/她有...	*tā/tā yǒu...*
blonde hair	金色的头发	*jīnsè de tóufǎ*
a knife	一把刀	*yī bǎ dāo*
He/She was...	他/她...	*tā/tā...*
tall	高个子	*gāo gèzi*
young	挺年青	*tǐng niánqīng*
short	矮个子	*ǎi gèzi*
He/She was wearing...	他/她穿着...	*tā/tā chuān zhe...*
jeans	牛仔服装	*niúzǎi fúzhuāng*
a red shirt	一件红衬衫	*yī jiàn hóng chènshān*

basic grammar

* measure words

In English, we sometimes use 'measure words' to modify certain nouns, for example 'piece' in 'a piece of cake' or 'pair' in 'a pair of trousers'. In Chinese, every noun, when preceded by a number or a demonstrative pronoun (e.g. 'this', 'that') must have a measure word inserted before it. Different measure words are used with different nouns. For example, běn is used in sān běn shū (three books), liàng is used in sān liàng che (three cars). Below are some of the most commonly used measure words:

CHARACTER	PINYIN	CATEGORY	EXAMPLE NOUNS
包	*bāo*	parcel, packet	books, biscuits
杯	*bēi*	cup, glass	coffee, beer
本	*běn*	volume	dictionary
个	*gè*	people	man, girl
家	*jiā*	organisation	company
块	*kuài*	square piece	soap
辆	*liàng*	things with wheels	bike, car
瓶	*píng*	bottle, jar	beer, jam
条	*tiáo*	long and winding	river
头	*tóu*	big animals	pig
张	*zhāng*	thin, flat	paper
只	*zhī*	small animals	chicken
座	*zuò*	solid	mountain

To get by in Chinese, the measure word gè (often pronounced with a neutral tone) can be used in most circumstances, so you will be understood if you say, for example, sān gè shū instead of sān běn shū. Measure words are not used in front of tiān (day) and nián (year). So, you say sān tiān (three days) and yī nián (one year).

* nouns and articles

Nouns in Chinese have no singular and plural distinctions. For example, the word shū remains the same whether you are talking about yī běn shū (one book) or shí běn shū (ten books). Chinese has no articles (words for 'a' and 'the'). So, Wǒ qù mǎi shū can mean 'I'm going to buy *a* book' or 'I'm going to buy *the* book'. The context and words such as yī běn (one) or zhè běn (this) will help to clarify the meaning.

* verbs

Verbs have only one form. For example, qù means 'to go to' and it is used in Wǒ qù Zhōngguó (I go to China), Tā qù Zhōngguó (He goes to China), Wǒmen qù Zhōngguó (We go to China), etc. Verbs do not change their forms to indicate past, present, future or continuous tenses.

* the past

A past event can be indicated by the particle le, which goes after the verb or at the end of the sentence: Tā qù le Zhōngguó (He's gone to China/He went to China). To say you have experienced something or you have been somewhere, put guò after the verb: Tā qù guò Zhōngguó (He's been to China).

To indicate where, when and how something happened in the past, put de after the verb or at the end of the sentence:

Wǒ wǔ nián qián láī de Yīngguó.
(I came to Britain five years ago.)
Lit. I five years ago came Britain.

Very often, shì (to be) is used with de for extra emphasis:

Wǒ shì wǔ nián qián láī Yīngguó de.
(It was five years ago that I came to Britain.)
Lit. I be five years ago came Britain.

However, the particles le, guò and de are not usually used with static verbs such as yǒu (to have), zhīdào (to know), shì (to be), xiāngxìng (to believe), etc. Time expressions and context make it clear whether you are talking about the past or present:

Sān nián qián tā shí dǎoyóu.
(He was a tourist guide three years ago.)
Lit. Three years ago he be tourist guide.

* the future

The future is usually indicated by time expressions, or by putting words like jiāng (shall) and yào (will) before the verb:

Wǒ míngnián qù Zhōngguó.
(I'm going to China next year.)
Lit. I next year go China.

Wǒ yào qù Zhōngguó.
(I'm going to China.)
Lit. I will go China.

* the continuous

Continuous actions are indicated by putting zài or zhèngzài before the verb:

	Wŏ	zài	kàn	diànshì.
	(I am watching TV)			
Lit.	I		watch	TV.

This can also mean 'I was watching TV' if used in the context of talking about the past, or with an expression like 'last night'.

* negatives

To make a sentence negative in Chinese, you simply put bù or méi before the verb. Bù is used in most sentences.

	Tā	bù	xǐhuān	Zhōngguó fàn.
	(He doesn't like Chinese food)			
Lit.	He	not	like	Chinese food.

Méi is used with the verb yŏu (to have), and to talk about events that haven't happened:

	Wŏ	méi	yŏu	Zhōngguó chá.
	(I don't have Chinese tea.)			
Lit.	I	not	have	Chinese tea.

	Tā	méi	qù	Zhōngguó.
	(He didn't go/hasn't gone to China)			
Lit.	He	not	go	China.

* adjectives and adverbs

Adjectives go before nouns, e.g. hǎo shū (a good book). If an adjective consists of two syllables, add de before the noun, e.g. piàoliang de shū (a beautiful book). You also add de if an adverb is used before the adjective, e.g. hěn hǎo de shū (a very good book).

* word order

The common patterns are:

- subject + verb + object
  Wǒ mǎi shū.
  (I buy a book.)

- subject + specific time + verb + object
  Tā liù diǎn chī wǎnfàn.
  (She has supper at six o'clock.)

- subject + verb + a period of time + object
  Tā kàn le yī gè xiǎoshí diànshì.
  (He watched TV for an hour.)

- subject + place + verb (+ object)
  Wǒ zài Běijīng gōngzuò.
  (I work in Beijing.)

- object + subject + verb (to emphasize the object)
  Xìn, wǒ xiě le.
  (That letter, I did write it.)

* questions

When asking specific questions using 'who?', 'when?' etc, the question word goes at the end of the sentence:

Nǐ jiào shénme?
(What's your name?)
Lit. You are called what?

To ask a yes or no question (e.g. Do you like it?) just add ma to the end of a sentence:

Tā shì Zhōngguóren ma?
(Is she Chinese?)
Lit. She is Chinese?

* yes and no

The Chinese equivalents for 'yes' and 'no' are shì de and bú shì, but they are not used as extensively as in English. In Chinese, to reply 'yes' or 'no' to a question, you usually repeat the verb used in the question to mean 'yes', adding bù before the verb to mean 'no'.
For example:

Nǐ xǐhuān Zhōngguó fàn ma?
(Do you like Chinese food?)
Lit. You like Chinese food?

Xǐhuān./Bù xǐhuān.
(Yes, I do./No, I don't.)
Lit. Like./Not like.

English – Chinese Dictionary

See **basic grammar**, page 167, for further explanation of Chinese nouns.

There's a list of **car parts** on page 72 and **parts of the body** on page 158. See also the **menu reader** on page 104, and **numbers** on page 18.

A

a, an 一个 *yīge*
ability 能力 *nénglì*
able 能 *néng*
about *(approximately)* 大约/左右 *dàyuē/zuǒyòu*
» *(relating to)* 关于 *guānyú*
above 在..... 上 *zài...shàng*
abroad 国外 *guówài*
to accept *(present)* 收下 *shōuxià*
»*(apologies)* 接受 *jiēshòu*
accident 事故 *shìgù*
accommodation 住宿 *zhùsù*
accountant 会计 *kuàijì*
ache 疼 *téng*
acid 酸 *suān*
across 穿过 *chuānguò*
to act 表演 *biǎoyǎn*
actor, actress 演员 *yǎnyuán*
acupuncture 针灸 *zhēnjiǔ*
adaptor 多路插座 *duōlù chāzuò*
addicted 上瘾 *shàngyǐn*
address 地址 *dìzhǐ*
admission *(to a park)* 入场 *rùchǎng*
to adopt *(children)* 收养 *shōuyǎng*
» *(opinion)* 采纳 *cǎinà*
adopted 收养的 *shōuyǎngde*
adult 成人 *chéngrén*
advance *(early payment)* 预支 *yùzhī*
» *(in advance)* 提前 *tíqián*
advanced *(technology)* 先进 *xiānjìn*
adventure 冒险 *màoxiǎn*
advertisement; advertising 广告 *guǎnggào*
advise 劝告 *quàngào*
aeroplane 飞机 *fēijī*
afford: I can't afford it 买不起 *mǎibùqǐ*
afraid: I'm afraid 恐怕 *kǒngpà*
after ....后 *....hòu*
afternoon 下午 *xiàwǔ*
afterwards 以后 *yǐhòu*
again 再 *zài*
against 反对 *fǎnduì*
age 年龄 *niánlíng*
agency 代理 *dàilǐ*
ago ....前 *....qián*
to agree 同意 *tóngyì*
agriculture 农业 *nóngyè*
AIDS 艾滋病 *àizībìng*
air: by air 坐飞机 *zuò fēijī*
Air China 中国民航 *zhōngguó mínháng*
air-conditioning 空调 *kōngtiáo*
airforce 空军 *kōngjūn*
airline 航空公司 *hángkōng gōngsī*
air mail 航空信 *hángkōng xìn*

airport 飞机场 *fēijīchǎng*
airport bus 民航班车 *mínháng bānchē*
aisle 走道 *zǒudào*
alarm clock 闹钟 *nàozhōng*
alcohol 酒 *jiǔ*
alcoholic *(person)* 酗酒的人 *xùjiǔ de rén*
alive 活着 *huózhe*
all 所有的 *suǒyǒude*
allergic to 对... 过敏 *duì...guòmǐn*
to allow 允许 *yǔnxǔ*
all right 行 *xíng*
alone 单独 *dāndú*
already 已经 *yǐjīng*
also 也 *yě*
to alter 改 *gǎi*
although 虽然 *suīrán*
altogether 一共 *yīgòng*
always 总是 *zǒngshì*
a.m. 上午 *shàngwǔ*
ambassador 大使 *dàshǐ*
ambitious 有抱负 *yǒubàofù*
ambulance 救护车 *jiùhù chē*
America 美国 *měiguó*
American *(people)* 美国人 *měiguórén*
among 在...当中 *zài... dāngzhōng*
amount 数量 *shùliàng*
amusement park 游乐园 *yóulè yuán*
anaesthetic 麻醉 *mázuì*
and 和 *hé*
angry 发怒 *fānù*
animal 动物 *dòngwù*
anniversary 周年 *zhōunián*
annoyed 生气 *shēngqì*
another 另一个 *lìngyīgè*
answer *(a reply)* 答复 *dáfù*
to answer *(question)* 回答 *huídá*
» *(telephone)* 接 *jiē*
antibiotic 抗菌素 *kàngjùnsù*
antique 古董 *gǔdǒng*
antiseptic 消炎 *xiāoyán*
anxious 着急 *zháojí*
any 任何 *rènhé*
anything 任何事 *rènhéshì*
anyway 反正 *fǎnzhèng*
anywhere 任何地方 *rènhé dìfāng*
apart from 除了 *chúle*
apartment 公寓 *gōngyù*
appendicitis 阑胃炎 *lánwèiyán*
to apologize 道歉 *dàoqiàn*
appointment 约会 *yuēhuì*
approximately 大约 *dàyuē*
archaeology 考古 *kǎogǔ*
architect 建筑师 *jiànzhúshī*
area code 地区号 *dìqū hào*
to argue 争论 *zhēnglùn*
argument 论点 *lùndiǎn*
aristocracy 贵族 *guìzú*
army 军队 *jūnduì*
around 周围 *zhōuwéi*
to arrange 安排 *ānpái*
arrest: under arrest 被逮捕 *bèi dǎibǔ*
arrival 到达/到站 *dàodá/dàozhàn*
to arrive 到达/到 *dàodá/dào*
art 艺术 *yìshù*
art and craft store 工艺美术商店 *gōngyì měishù shāngdiàn*
art gallery 美术馆 *měishù guǎn*
arthritis 关节炎 *guānjiéyán*
article *(essay)* 文章 *wénzhāng*
artificial 人造的 *rénzàode*
artist 艺术家 *yìshùjiā*
as 作为 *zuòwéi*
ashtray 烟灰缸 *yānhuīgāng*
to ask 问 *wèn*
aspirin 阿斯匹林 *āsīpǐlín*
assistant 助手 *zhùshǒu*
asthma 哮喘 *xiāochuǎn*
at 在 *zài*
athlete 运动员 *yùndòngyuán*

athletics 田径运动 *tiánjìng yùndòng*
atmosphere 气氛 *qìfēn*
to attack 袭击 *xíjí*
attractive 漂亮/迷人 *piāoliàng/mírén*
auction 拍卖 *pāimài*
Australia 澳大利亚 *àodàlìyà*
Australian 澳大利亚人 *àodàlìyàrén*
author 作家 *zuòjiā*
automatic 自动 *zìdòng*
avalanche 雪崩 *xuěbēng*
to avoid 避免 *bìmiǎn*
to be awake 醒了 *xǐng le*
away 出门了 *chūmén le*
awful 糟透了 *zāotòu le*

B

baby 婴儿 *yīng'ér*
baby's bottle 婴儿奶瓶 *yīng'ér nǎipíng*
babysitter 保姆 *bǎomǔ*
back *(reverse side)* 反面 *fǎnmiàn*
backwards 落后 *luòhòu*
bad 坏/糟糕 *huài/zāogāo*
bad at... 不好 *bù hǎo*
bag 包 *bāo*
baggage 行李 *xínglǐ*
bakery 面包屋 *miànbāo wū*
balcony 阳台 *yángtái*
bald 秃顶 *tūdǐng*
ball 球 *qiú*
ballet 芭蕾 *bāléi*
ballpoint pen 圆珠笔 *yuánzhū bǐ*
bamboo 竹子 *zhúzi*
band *(music)* 小乐队 *xiǎoyuèduì*
bandage 包扎 *bāozā*
bank 银行 *yínháng*
banker 银行家 *yínhángjiā*
Bank of China 中国银行 *zhōngguó yínháng*
bar 酒吧 *jiǔbā*
barbecued 烧烤 *shāokǎo*
barber's 理发店 *lǐfà diàn*
bargain 合算 *hésuàn*
baseball 磊球 *lěiqiú*
basement 地下室 *dìxiàshì*
basin 洗手池 *xǐshǒuchí*
basket 篮子 *lánzi*
basketball 篮球 *lánqiú*
bath 洗澡 *xǐzǎo*
bathing costume 游泳衣 *yóuyǒng yī*
bathroom 卫生间 *wèishēng jiān*
bath towel 浴巾 *yùjīn*
battery 电池 *diànchí*
to be *(am, is, are)* 是 *shì*
beach 海滩/沙滩 *hǎitān/shātān*
beard 胡子 *húzi*
beautiful 美 *měi*
because 因为 *yīnwéi*
to become 当/成为 *dāng/chéngwéi*
bed 床 *chuáng*
bedroom 卧室 *wòshì*
bee 蜜蜂 *mìfēng*
before 从前;...前 *cóngqián; ... qián*
to begin 开始 *kāishǐ*
beginner 初学者 *chūxué zhě*
behind 后面 *hòumiàn*
Beijing (Peking) Opera 京剧 *jīngjù*
beige 米色 *mǐsè*
to believe 相信 *xiāngxìn*
bell 铃 *ling*
belong 属于 *shǔyú*
below 在...下面 *zài... xiàmiàn*
belt 皮带 *pídài*
to bend 弯曲 *wānqū*
berth 铺 *pù*
beside 在...旁边 *zài...pángbiān*
best 最好 *zuìhǎo*
better 更好 *gènghǎo*
better than... 比.... 好 *bǐ...hǎo*
between 在.... 之间 *zài...zhījiān*
beware 注意/当心 *zhùyì/dāngxīn*

beyond 在…以外 *zài...yǐwài*
bib 围嘴 *wéizuǐ*
Bible 圣经 *shèngjīng*
bicycle 自行车 *zìxíngchē*
big 大 *dà*
bigger 更大 *gèngdà*
bill 帐单 *zhàngdān*
bin 垃圾箱 *lājī xiāng*
binding 装订 *zhuāngdìng*
binoculars 望远镜 *wàngyuǎnjìng*
biology 生物学 *shēngwùxué*
bird 鸟 *niǎo*
birthday 生日 *shēngrì*
bishop 主教 *zhǔjiào*
bit: a bit 一点 *yīdiǎn*
to bite 咬/叮 *yǎo/dīng*
bitter 苦 *kǔ*
black 黑色 *hēisè*
black and white 黑白 *hēi bái*
blade 刀片 *dāopiàn*
blanket 毯子 *tǎnzi*
to bleach 漂白 *piāobái*
to bleed 流血 *liúxiě*
blind *(person)* 盲人 *mángrén*
blister 水泡/泡 *shuǐpào/pào*
to block 堵塞 *dǔsè*
blocked 堵住了 *dǔzhù le*
blonde 金发 *jīnfà*
blood 血 *xiě*
blood type 血型 *xiě xíng*
blouse 女式上衣 *nǚshì shàngyī*
to blow 吹 *chuī*
to blow-dry 吹干 *chuī gān*
blue 蓝色 *lánsè*
to board *(aeroplane)* 上/登 *shàng/ dēng*
boarding gate 凳机口 *dèngjī kǒu*
boat 船 *chuán*
body 身子 *shēnzi*
to boil 烧开 *shāokāi*
boiled egg 煮鸡蛋 *zhǔ jīdàn*
boiled rice 白米饭 *bái mǐfàn*
boiling water, boiled water 开水 *kāi shuǐ*
bomb 炸弹 *zhádàn*
bone 骨头 *gútou*
book 书 *shū*
to book 订 *dìng*
booking office 订票处 *dìngpiào chǔ*
bookshop 书店 *shūdiàn*
boots 靴子 *xuēzi*
border *(of a country)* 边境 *biānjìng*
boring 没意思 *méi yìsī*
to borrow 借 *Jiè*
both 两; 都 *Liǎng; dōu*
bottle 瓶子 *píngzi*
bottle-opener 开瓶刀 *kāipíng dāo*
bottom 底; 最底下 *dǐ; zuìdǐxià*
to bow 鞠躬 *júgōng*
bow tie 花领结 *huā lǐngjié*
bowl 碗 *wǎn*
box 盒子 *hézi*
box lunch 盒饭 *hé fàn*
box office 票房 *piào fáng*
boy 男孩 *nánhái*
boyfriend 男朋友 *nán péngyǒu*
bra 胸罩 *xiōngzhào*
bracelet 手镯 *shǒuzhuó*
brand 商标/牌子 *shāngbiāo/páizi*
brass 黄铜 *huáng tóng*
brave 勇敢 *yǒnggǎn*
bread 面包 *miànbāo*
to break 弄断 *nòng duàn*
to break down 坏了 *huài le*
breakfast 早饭 *zǎofàn*
to breathe 呼吸 *hūxī*
brick 砖 *zhuān*
bride 新娘 *xīnniáng*
bridegroom 新郎 *xīnláng*
bridge 桥 *qiáo*
» *(game)* 桥牌 *qiáopái*
briefcase 手提箱 *shǒutí xiāng*
bright 亮/明亮 *liàng/míngliàng*

to bring 带来/带 *dàilái/dài*
Britain 英国 *yīngguó*
British *(people)* 英国人 *yīngguórén*
broad 宽 *kuān*
brochure 说明书 *shuōmíngshū*
broken 断了; 摔坏了 *duàn le; shuāihuài le*
bronchitis 气管炎 *qìguǎnyán*
bronze 青铜 *qīngtóng*
brooch 胸针 *xiōngzhēn*
broom 扫帚 *sǎozhǒu*
brother *(younger)* 弟弟 *dìdi*
» *(elder)* 哥哥 *gēge*
brown 棕色/褐色 *zōngsè/hésè*
bruise 擦伤 *cāshāng*
brush 刷子 *shuāzi*
to brush 刷 *shuā*
bucket 桶 *tǒng*
Buddha 佛 *fó*
Buddhism 佛教 *fójiào*
Buddhist 佛教徒 *fójiàotú*
Buddhist temple 佛教寺院 *fójiào sìyuàn*
budget 预算 *yùsuàng*
buffet 自助餐 *zìzhùcān*
to build 建/盖 *jiàn/gài*
builder 建筑工人 *jiànzhú gōngrén*
building 大楼 *dàlóu*
bulb 灯泡 *dēngpào*
burned 焦了 *jiāo le*
bus 公共汽车/巴士 *gōnggòng qìchē/bāshì*
bus stop 公共汽车站 *gōnggòng qìchē zhàn*
to be on business 出差 *chūchāi*
business card 名片 *míngpiàn*
business class 商务舱 *shāngwù cāng*
businessman/woman 商人 *shāngrén*
busy 忙 *máng*
but 但是 *dànshì*
butcher's 肉店 *ròu diàn*
butter 黄油 *huángyóu*
button 扣子 *kòuzi*
to buy 买 *mǎi*
by: by the end of 在...之前 *zài... zhīqián*
by myself 我自己 *wǒ zìjǐ*

C

cabin 机舱 *jīcāng*
cable car 缆车 *lǎn chē*
café 咖啡厅 *kāfēi tīng*
calculator 计算器 *jìsuànqì*
calendar 日历 *rìlì*
to call, to be called 叫 *jiào*
calligraphy 书法 *shūfǎ*
calm 沉着/冷静 *chénzhuó/lěngjìng*
to calm down 别着急/冷静下来 *bié zháojí/lěngjìng xiàlai*
camera 照相机 *zhàoxiàngjī*
to camp 露营 *lùyíng*
can *(to be able to)* 能/会 *néng/huì*
» *(tin)* 罐头 *guàntóu*
Canada 加拿大 *jiānádà*
to cancel 取消 *qǔ xiāo*
cancer 癌症 *áizhèng*
candle 蜡烛 *làzhú*
canoe 独木舟 *dúmùzhōu*
can opener 开罐头刀 *kāi guàntóu dāo*
Cantonese *(dialect)* 广东话 *guǎngdōnghuà*
Cantonese food 粤菜 *yuè cài*
capital *(city)* 首都 *shǒudū*
car 车 *chē*
cards 卡片/牌 *kǎpiàn/pái*
cardigan 开衫毛衣 *kāishān máoyī*
to take care 照顾 *zhào gù*
career 职业/工作 *zhíyè/gōngzuò*
careful 当心 *dāngxīn*
careless 不当心 *búdāngxīn*
carpenter 木工 *mùgōng*

carpet 地毯 *dìtǎn*
carriage *(train)* 车厢 *chēxiāng*
carrier bag 手提袋 *shǒutí dài*
to carry 带/提 *dài/tí*
to carry on 继续 *jìxù*
cartoon 动画片 *dònghuàpiàn*
case: in case 万一 *wànyī*
cash 现金 *xiànjīn*
cashier 收款人 *shōukuǎnrén*
castle 城堡 *chéngbǎo*
cat 猫 *māo*
catalogue 目录 *mùlù*
to catch *(thief)* 抓 *zhuā*
» *(train/bus)* 赶 *gǎn*
cathedral 大教堂 *dàjiàotáng*
Catholic 天主教 *tiānzhǔjiào*
cause *(reason)* 原因 *yuányīn*
to cause 引起 *yǐnqǐ*
caution 当心 *dāngxīn*
cave 山洞 *shāndòng*
CD 光盘 *guāngpán*
CD-Rom 多媒体光盘 *duōméitǐ guāngpán*
cavity *(teeth)* 牙洞 *yádòng*
ceiling 天花板 *tiānhuābǎn*
celebration 庆祝 *qìngzhù*
celebrity 名人 *míngrén*
cellar 地窖 *dìjiào*
cemetery 墓地 *mùdì*
centimetre 厘米 *límǐ*
centre 中心 *zhōngxīn*
century 世纪 *shìjì*
CEO 公司总裁 *gōngsī zǒngcái*
ceramics 陶瓷 *táocí*
cereal: breakfast cereal 早餐麦片 *zǎocān màipiàn*
certain: not certain 不一定 *bù yīdìng*
certainly 当然 *dāngrán*
certificate 证书 *zhèngshū*
chain 链子 *liànzi*
chair 椅子 *y zi*
chairman 主席 *zhǔxí*
champagne 香槟 *xiāngbīn*
chance 机会/机遇 *jīhuì/ jīyù*
change *(coin)* 零钱 *língqián*
to change *(money/clothes)* 换 *huàn*
changing room 更衣室 *gēngyī shì*
character *(in a film)* 人物 *rénwù*
» *(personality)* 性格 *xìnggé*
» *(Chinese character)* 字 *zì*
charger *(phone)* 充电器 *chōngdiànqì*
charming 迷人 *mírén*
to chat 聊天 *liáotiān*
cheap 便宜 *piányí*
to cheat 骗 *piàn*
checked *(pattern)* 格子 *gézi*
to check in *(at airport)* 办理登机手续 *bànlǐ dēngjī shǒuxù*
» *(at hotel)* 办理住宿手续 *bànlǐ zhùsù shǒuxù*
to check out *(at hotel)* 办理离开手续 *bànlǐ líkāi shǒuxù*
cheeky 厚脸皮 *hòuliǎnpí*
Cheers! 干杯 *gān bēi*
chef 厨师 *chúshī*
chemist's 药店 *yàodiàn*
chess 象棋 *xiàngqí*
chewing gum 口香糖 *kǒuxiāng táng*
chicken 鸡 *jī*
chickenpox 水豆 *shuǐdòu*
child, children 孩子/小孩/儿童 *háizi/xiǎohái/értóng*
chilli 辣椒/辣子 *làjiāo/làzi*
chimney 烟囱 *yāncōng*
chin 下巴 *xiàbā*
China 中国 *zhōngguó*
Chinese *(language)* 中文/汉语 *zhōngwén/ hànyǔ*
» *(people)* 中国人 *zhōngguórén*
Chinese medicine 中药 *zhōngyào*
Chinese tea 中国茶 *zhōngguó chá*

Chinese traditional medicine doctor 中医 *zhōngyī*
Chinese Sichuan pepper 花椒 *huājiāo*
to choose 挑/选 *tiāo/xuǎn*
chopsticks 筷子 *kuàizi*
Christian 基督教 *jīdūjiào*
Christmas 圣诞节 *shèngdànjié*
church 教堂 *jiàotáng*
cigar 雪茄烟 *xuějiāyān*
cigarette 香烟 *xiāngyān*
cinema 电影院 *diànyǐngyuàn*
circle 圆圈 *yuánquān*
citizen 公民 *gōngmín*
city 城市 *chéngshì*
civil servant 公务员 *gōng wù yuán*
class *(social group)* 阶层 *jiēcéng*
classical 古典 *gǔdiǎn*
claustrophobia 幽闭恐怖症 *yōubì kǒngbù zhèng*
clean 干净 *gānjìng*
to clean 打扫/清扫 *dǎsǎo/qīngsǎo*
clerk 职员 *zhíyuán*
clever 聪明 *cōngmíng*
client 客户 *kèhù*
cliff 悬崖 *xuányá*
climate 气候 *qìhòu*
to climb 爬 *pá*
clinic 诊所/医务所 *zhěnsuǒ/yīwùsuǒ*
cloakroom 存衣室 *cúnyīshì*
clock 钟 *zhōng*
to close 关 *guān*
to be closed 近 *jìn*
cloth 布 *bù*
clothes 衣服 *yīfú*
clothing 服装 *fúzhuāng*
cloudy 多云 *duōyún*
club 俱乐部 *jūlèbù*
coach *(long distance bus)* 长途车 *chángtúchē*
coal 煤炭 *méitàn*
coast 海边 *hǎibiān*
coat 大衣 *dàyī*
coat hanger 衣架 *yījià*
Coca-Cola 可口可乐 *kěkǒu kělè*
cocktail 鸡尾酒 *jīwěijiǔ*
coffee 咖啡 *kāfēi*
coin 硬币 *yìngbì*
cold 冷 *lěng*
to have a cold 感冒 *gǎnmào*
collaboration 合作 *hézuò*
collar 领子 *lǐngzi*
colleague 同事 *tóngshì*
collection 收藏 *shōucáng*
college 学院 *xuéyuàn*
colour 颜色 *yánsè*
comb 梳子 *shūzi*
to come 来 *lái*
comedy 喜剧 *xǐjù*
comfortable 舒服 *shūfú*
comic 滑稽 *huájī*
commemorative 纪念 *jìniàn*
commercial 商业 *shāngyè*
commercial *(ads)* 广告 *guǎnggào*
common *(ordinary)* 一般 *yībān*
» *(public)* 公用 *gōngyòng*
communism 共产主义 *gòngchǎn zhǔyì*
to commute 乘车上班 *chéngchē shàngbān*
company 公司 *gōngsī*
to compare 对比/比较 *duìbǐ/ bǐjiào*
compared with 和... 相比 *hé... xiāngbǐ*
to complain; complaint 抱怨/埋怨 *bàoyuàn/máiyuàn*
complete *(finished)* 完成了 *wánchéngle*
» *(whole)* 全体 *quántǐ*
completely 完全 *wánquán*
complicated 复杂 *fùzá*
composer 作曲家 *zuòqūjiā*

to compromise 让步 *ràngbù*
compulsory 必须的 *bìxūde*
computer 电脑/计算机 *diànnǎo/jìsuànjī*
computer programmer 电脑程序编写者 *diànnǎo chéngxù biānxiě zhě*
computer science 电脑科学 *diànnǎo kēxué*
concert 音乐会 *yīnyuèhuì*
concert hall 音乐大厅 *yīnyuè dàtīng*
concussion 脑振荡 *nǎozhèndàng*
condition 条件 *tiáojiàn*
conditioner 护发素 *hùfàsù*
condom 避孕套 *bìyùntào*
conference 会议/大会 *huìyì/dàhuì*
conference room 会议室 *huìyì shì*
to confirm 确认 *quèrèn*
to congratulate 祝贺 *zhùhè*
Congratulations! 恭喜 *gōngxǐ*
conjunctivitis 结膜炎 *jiémóyán*
connection 连接 *liánjiē*
conscious 清醒 *qīngxǐng*
conservation 保护 *bǎohù*
conservative 保守 *bǎoshǒu*
to consider 考虑 *kǎolǜ*
constipation 便秘 *biàn mì*
consulate 领事馆 *lǐngshìguǎn*
consultant 咨询顾问 *zīxún gùwèn*
to contact 与... 联系 *yǔ...liánxì*
contact lens 隐形眼镜 *yǐnxíng yǎnjìng*
contact lens cleaner 隐形眼镜清洁剂 *yǐnxíng yǎnjìng qīngjiéjì*
contact name 联系人 *liánxì rén*
continent 洲 *zhōu*
to continue 继续 *jìxù*
contraceptive 避孕 *bìyùn*
contract 合同 *hétóng*
to control 控制 *kòngzhì*
convenient 方便 *fāngbiàn*
conversation 对话/谈话 *duìhuà/tánhuà*
to cook 做饭 *zuò fàn*
cooker: rice cooker 电饭煲 *diàn fànbāo*
cool 凉 *liáng*
copper 铜 *tóng*
to copy 抄下来 *chāo xiàlái*
corkscrew 螺丝瓶起子 *luósī píngqǐzi*
corn 玉米 *yùmǐ*
corner 角落 *jiǎoluò*
correct 对/正确 *duì/zhèngquè*
corridor 走廊 *zǒuláng*
to cost 花 *huā*
cot 婴儿床 *yīngér chuáng*
cotton: 100% cotton 纯棉 *chúnmián*
cotton wool 棉花球 *miánhuāqiú*
to cough 咳嗽 *késòu*
could 可以 *kěyǐ*
counselling 咨询 *zīxún*
to count *(number)* 数 *shǔ*
country 国家 *guójiā*
countryside 农村 *nóngcūn*
couple *(a pair)* 一对儿 *yīduìr*
» *(married)* 夫妻 *fūqī*
courage 勇气 *yǒngqì*
cow 母牛 *mǔniú*
crab 螃蟹 *pángxiè*
to crash 相撞 *xiāngzhuàng*
crazy 发疯 *fāfēng*
credit card 信用卡 *xìnyòng kǎ*
crispy 脆 *cuì*
cross: be cross 生气 *shēngqì*
to cross 过/越过 *guò/ yuèguò*
crossroad 十字路口 *shízì lùkǒu*
crowd 一群人 *yīqúnrén*
crowded 拥挤/挤 *yōngjǐ/ jǐ*
cruise 游艇 *yóutǐng*
to cry 哭 *kū*
crystal 水晶 *shuǐjīng*
cucumber 黄瓜 *huángguā*

cuff 袖口 *xiùkǒu*
cuisine 烹调 *pēngtiáo*
culture 文化 *wénhuà*
cup 杯子 *bēizi*
cupboard 柜子 *guìzi*
cure *(remedy)* 治疗办法 *zhìliáo bànfǎ*
to cure 治疗 *zhìliáo*
curly 卷曲 *juǎnqū*
currency 货币 *huòbì*
current *(electrical)* 电流 *diànliú*
» *(recent)* 当前 *dāngqián*
curry 咖喱 *gālī*
curtain 窗帘 *chuānglián*
curve 斜线 *xiéxiàn*
cushion 靠垫 *kàodiàn*
customer 顾客 *gùkè*
to cut 切开/切 *qiēkāi/ qiē*
cut *(wound)* 口子 *kǒuzi*
cutlery 餐具 *cānjù*
to cycle, cycling 骑车 *qíchē*
cystitis 膀胱炎 *pǎngguāng yán*

D

dad 爸爸, 爹 *bàba, diē*
daily 每天 *měitiān*
to damage 损坏/弄坏 *sǔnhuài/ nònghuài*
damp 潮湿 *cháoshī*
to dance 跳舞 *tiàowǔ*
dancer 舞蹈家 *wǔdǎojiā*
danger 危险 *wéixiǎn*
dangerous 危险的 *wéixiǎnde*
dark *(night)* 黑 *hēi*
» *(colour)* 深 *shēn*
darling 亲爱的 *qīnàide*
date 日期 *rìqī*
date of birth 出生日期 *chū shēng rìqī*
daughter 女儿 *nǚ'ér*
daughter-in-law 儿媳妇/儿媳 *ér xífù/ér xí*
day 天 *tiān*
» day after tomorrow 后天 *hòu tiān*
» day before yesterday 前天 *qián tiān*
dead 死 *sǐ*
deaf 聋 *lóng*
death 死亡 *sǐwáng*
debt 债 *zhài*
decaffeinated 不含咖啡因 *bùhán kāfēiyīn*
deck *(of a ship)* 甲板 *jiǎbǎn*
to decide, decision 决定 *juèdìng*
to declare 宣布 *xuānbù*
deep 深 *shēn*
to deep-fry 炸 *zhá*
deer 鹿 *lù*
defect 缺点 *quēdiǎn*
defective 有缺陷的 *yǒu quēxiàn de*
to defrost 除霜 *chú shuāng*
degree *(angle)* 角度 *jiǎodù*
» *(temperature)* 度 *dù*
» *(university)* 学位 *xuéwèi*
to delay 推迟/延迟 *tuīchí/yánchí*
delicate *(matter)* 微妙 *wéimiào*
» *(fragile)* 易碎的 *yìsuìde*
delicious 好吃/香 *hǎochī/xiāng*
to deliver 送 *sòng*
delivery 送货 *sònghuò*
demonstration 游行 *yóuxíng*
denim 劳动布 *láodòngbù*
dentist 牙医 *yáyī*
denture 假牙 *jiǎyá*
deodorant 腋下喷剂 *yèxià pēnjì*
to depart 离开 *líkāi*
department *(academic)* 系 *xì*
» *(corporate)* 部门 *bùmén*
department store 百货商店 *bǎihuò shāngdiàn*
departure *(flight)* 离港/离开 *lígǎng/líkāi*
» *(train)* 发车/开车 *fāchē/kāichē*
to depend 靠 *kào*

» it depends 看情况 *kàn qíngkuàng*
deposit 押金 *yājīn*
to describe, description 描述 *miáoshù*
design, to design 设计 *shèjì*
desk 桌子 *zhuōzi*
dessert 甜点 *tiándiǎn*
destination 目的地/终点 *mùdìdì/zhōngdiǎn*
detail 细节 *xìjié*
detailed 详细 *xiángxì*
detergent 洗涤剂 *xǐdíjì*
to develop *(film)* 冲洗 *chōngxǐ*
diabetes 糖尿病 *tángniàobìng*
diabetic 有糖尿病的 *yǒu tángniàobìng de*
to dial 拨号 *bōhào*
dialling code 电话区号 *diànhuà qūhào*
dialling tone 拨号音 *bōhào yīn*
diamond 钻石 *zuànshí*
diarrhoea 拉肚子/闹肚子 *lā dùzi/nào dùzi*
diary 日记 *rìjì*
dice 骰子 *shǎizi*
dictator 独裁者 *dúcáizhě*
dictionary 字典/词典 *zìdiǎn/cídiǎn*
to die 死 *sǐ*
diesel 柴油 *cháiyóu*
diet 日常饮食 *rìcháng yǐnshí*
difference 不同 *bùtóng*
different 不同的 *bùtóngde*
difficult 难 *nán*
difficulty 困难 *kùnnán*
digital 数码 *shùmǎ*
dilemma 困境 *kùnjìng*
dim-sum 早茶 *zǎochá*
dining car 餐车 *cānchē*
dining room 餐厅 *cāntīng*
dinner 晚餐 *wǎncān*
diplomat 外交官 *wàijiāoguān*
direct 直接 *zhíjiē*
direction 方向 *fāngxiàng*
dirty 脏 *zāng*
disabled 残疾 *cánjí*
to disagree 不同意 *bùtóngyì*
disappointed 失望的 *shīwàngde*
disappointing 令人失望的 *lìngrén shīwàngde*
disco 迪斯科 *dísīkē*
discount 打折 *dǎzhé*
disease 疾病 *jíbìng*
dish *(container)* 碗 *wǎn*
» *(food)* 菜 *cài*
dishwasher 洗碗机 *xǐwǎnjī*
disinfectant 消毒剂 *xiāodújì*
disposable 一次性 *yīcìxìng*
distance 距离 *jùlí*
district 区 *qū*
to disturb 打扰 *dǎrǎo*
to dive 潜水 *qiánshuǐ*
diversion (road) 绕道 *ràodào*
diving 潜水的 *qiánshuǐde*
divorced 离婚了 *líhūnle*
dizzy 晕 *yūn*
to do 干/做 *gàn/zuò*
doctor 医生/大夫 *yīshēng/dàifū*
document 文件 *wénjiàn*
dog 狗 *gǒu*
doll 洋娃娃 *yángwáwá*
dollar *(Hong Kong)* 港币 *gǎngbì*
» *(US)* 美元 *měiyuán*
domestic 国内 *guónèi*
door *(train, car)* 车门 *chēmén*
double 双 *shuāng*
double bed 双人床 *shuāngrén chuáng*
double room 双人房间 *shuāngrén fángjiān*
down 下面 *xiàmiàn*
to download 下载 *xiàzài*
downstairs 楼下 *lóuxià*
drain 下水道 *xiàshuǐdào*

draught *(air)* 对流风 *duìliúfēng*
» *(beer)* 鲜啤酒/扎啤 *xiānpíjiǔ/zhāpí*
to draw *(in gambling)* 抽奖 *chōujiǎng*
to draw 抽 *chōu*
drawer 抽屉 *chōutì*
drawing 画 *huà*
dreadful 差劲儿/糟透了 *chājìnr/zāotòule*
dress *(clothes)* 长裙 *chángqún*
dressing *(salad)* 调料 *tiáoliào*
» *(medical)* 敷料 *fūliào*
drink 饮料 *yǐnliào*
to drink 喝 *hē*
drinking *(water)* 饮用水 *yǐnyòngshuǐ*
to drive 驾/开 *jià/kāi*
driver 司机 *sījī*
driving licence 驾驶执照 *jiàshǐ zhízhào*
to drown 淹死 *yānsǐ*
to drop 掉 *diào*
drug *(medication)* 药品 *yàopǐn*
drug addict 吸毒者 *xīdú zhě*
drunk 醉 *zuì*
dry 干 *gān*
dry cleaner's 干洗店 *gānxǐ diàn*
dubbed 配音的 *pèiyīnde*
duck 鸭 *yā*
due to 由于 *yóuyú*
dull *(boring)* 没意思 *méiyìsī*
dummy *(baby's)* 奶嘴 *nǎizuǐ*
dumpling 饺子 *jiǎozi*
during 在...期间 *zài...qījiān*
dustbin 簸箕 *bòjī*
dusty 灰 *huī*
duty *(obligation)* 责任 *zérèn*
» *(tax)* 税 *shuì*
duty-free 免税 *miǎn shuì*
duvet 被子 *bèizi*
DVD player DVD机 *DVD jī*
dynasty 朝代/朝 *cháodài/cháo*
dyslexia 诵读障碍 *sòngdú zhàng'ài*
dyslexic 诵读困难的 *sòngdú kùnnánde*

E

each 每个 *měige*
each other 互相 *hù xiāng*
ear infection 肿耳炎 *zhǒng'ěr yán*
early 早 *zǎo*
to earn 赚 *zhuàn*
earring 耳环 *ěrhuán*
earthquake 地震 *dìzhèn*
east 东 *dōng*
Easter 复活节 *fùhuójié*
eastern 东方的 *dōngfāngde*
easy 容易 *róngyì*
to eat 吃 *chī*
economical 经济的/省钱的 *jīngjìde/shěngqiánde*
economics 经济学 *jīngjìxué*
economy 经济 *jīngjì*
economy-class 经济舱 *jīngjì-cāng*
edible 可以吃的 *kěyǐchīde*
education 教育 *jiàoyù*
eel 鳝鱼 *shànyú*
egg fried-rice 蛋炒饭 *dàn chǎo-fàn*
elastic 松紧 *sōngjǐn*
election 选举 *xuǎnjǔ*
electrical 电 *diàn*
electrician 电工 *diàngōng*
electricity 电 *diàn*
electronic 电子 *diànzǐ*
email 电子邮件 *diànzǐ yóujiàn*
to email 发电子邮件 *fā diànzǐ yóujiàn*
to embark *(boat)* 上 *shàng*
embarrassing 发窘/尴尬 *fājiǒng/gāngà*
embassy 大使馆 *dàshǐguǎn*
emergency *(in hospital)* 急诊 *jízhēn*
emergency exit 紧急出口 *jǐnjí chūkǒu*
emperor 皇帝 *huángdì*

employee 雇员 *gùyuán*
employer 雇主 *gùzhǔ*
employment 就业 *jiùyè*
empress 女皇 *nǚhuáng*
empty 空 *kōng*
to end 结束 *jiéshù*
engaged *(marriage)* 订婚了 *dìnghūnle*
» *(telephone)* 占线 *zhànxiàn*
engine 发动机 *fādòngjī*
engineer 工程师 *gōngchéngshī*
England 英格兰 *yīnggélán*
English *(language)* 英语 *yīngyǔ*
to enjoy 享受; 喜欢 *xiǎngshòu; xǐhuān*
enough 足够 *zúgòu*
enquiries 问讯处 *wènxùnchǔ*
to enter 进入/进 *jìnrù/jìn*
entertainment 娱乐 *yúlè*
enthusiastic 热情 *rèqíng*
entrance 进口/入口 *jìnkǒu/rùkǒu*
envelope 信封 *xìnfēng*
environment 环境 *huánjìng*
environmentally friendly 对环境有益的 *duì huánjìng yǒuyìde*
equal 平等 *píngděng*
equipment 设备 *shèbèi*
escalator 电梯 *diàntī*
to escape 逃跑 *táopǎo*
especially 特别/格外 *tèbié/géwài*
estimate 估计数 *gūjìshù*
Euro 欧元 *ōuyuán*
Europe 欧洲 *ōuzhōu*
even *(number)* 双 *shuāng*
even if 既使 *jìshǐ*
evening 晚上 *wǎnshàng*
event 事件 *shìjiàn*
every 每, 每个 *měi, měige*
every day 每天 *měi tiān*
everyone 每个人 *měigerén*
everything 一切, 所有的 *yīqiē, suǒyǒude*
everywhere 每个地方, 到处 *měige dìfāng, dàochù*
exactly 确实 *quèshí*
examination 考试 *kǎoshì*
example: for example 比如 *bǐ rú*
to exceed 超过 *chāoguò*
excellent 优秀/出色 *yōuxiù/chūsè*
except 除了 *chúle*
to exchange 交换 *jiāohuàn*
exchange rate 对换率 *duìhuàn lǜ*
excited, exciting 激动 *jīdòng*
excursion 郊游 *jiāoyóu*
excuse me 对不起/劳驾 *duìbùqǐ/láojià*
to execute 枪毙 *qiāngbì*
executive (adj.) 执行的 *zhíxíngde*
to exercise *(body)* 锻炼 *duànliàn*
exhausted 累死了 *lèisǐle*
exhibition 展览 *zhǎnlǎn*
exit 出口 *chūkǒu*
to expect 期待 *qīdài*
expense 费用 *fèiyòng*
expensive 贵 *guì*
to experience 经历 *jīnglì*
experienced 有经验的 *yǒu jīngyànde*
experiment 实验, 试验 *shíyàn, shìyàn*
expert 专家 *zhuānjiā*
to explain, explanation 解释 *jiěshì*
explosion 爆炸 *bàozhá*
export, to export 出口 *chūkǒu*
to express 表达 *biǎodá*
express train 特快火车 *tèkuài huǒchē*
expression (facial) 表情 *biǎoqíng*
» (phrase) 表达法 *biǎodáfǎ*
extension (telephone) 分机 *fēnjī*
external 外部 *wàibù*
eyebrow 眉毛 *méimáo*
eyelash 眼睫毛 *yǎnjiémáo*
eyeliner 眼线笔 *yǎnxiànbǐ*
eyeshadow 眼影 *yǎnyǐng*

F

fabric 布料 *bùliào*
facilities 设施 *shèshī*
fact 事实 *shìshí*
in fact 事实上/说实话 *shìshíshàng/ shuō shíhuà*
factory 工厂 *gōngchǎng*
to fail *(exam, test)* 没通过/没及格 *méi tōngguò/méi jígé*
failure 失败 *shībài*
to fade *(colour)* 退色 *tuìsè*
to faint 晕倒 *yūndǎo*
fair *(just)* 公平 *gōngpíng*
» *(light colour)* 浅色 *qiǎnsè*
fairly 挺/比较 *tǐng/bǐjiào*
faith 信仰 *xìnyǎng*
faithful 衷诚 *zhōngchéng*
fake 假的 *jiǎde*
to fall in love 爱上了 *àishàngle*
false 假的 *jiǎde*
family 家庭 *jiātíng*
family name 姓 *xìng*
famous 有名/著名 *yǒumíng/zhùmíng*
fan *(air)* 扇子 *shànzi*
» *(supporter)* 迷 *mí*
fantastic 太棒了 *tàibàngle*
far away 远 *yuǎn*
fare 票价 *piàojià*
farm 农场 *nóngchǎng*
farmer 农场主 *nóngchǎngzhǔ*
fashion 时装 *shízhuāng*
fashionable 时髦 *shímáo*
fast 快 *kuài*
fast food 快餐 *kuài cān*
fat (adj.) 胖 *pàng*
» (noun) 脂肪 *zhīfáng*
fatal 致命 *zhìmìng*
father 父亲 *fùqīn*
father-in-law 公公, 岳父 *gōnggong, yuèfù*
fault 错误 *cuòwù*
faulty 次品/有问题 *cìpǐn/yǒu wèntí*
favourite (adj.) 喜爱的 *xǐ'àide*
fax 传真 *chuánzhēn*
fee 费 *fèi*
to feed 喂 *wèi*
to feel 感觉 *gǎnjué*
female 女的 *nǚde*
feminine 女性 *nǚxìng*
feminist 女权主义者 *nǚquán zhǔyìzhě*
ferry 轮渡 *lúndù*
festival 节日 *jiérì*
to fetch 取 *qǔ*
fever 发烧 *fāshāo*
few 少许/几个 *shǎoxǔ/jǐge*
fiancé 未婚夫 *wèihūnfū*
fiancée 未婚妻 *wèihūnqī*
field *(academic)* 领域 *lǐngyù*
» *(sport)* 场地 *chǎngdì*
fight 打架 *dǎjià*
figure 数字 *shùzì*
file *(document)* 文件 *wénjiàn*
to fill 填, 补 *tián, bǔ*
filling *(food)* 馅儿 *xiànr*
» *(tooth)* 填牙料 *tiányáliào*
film *(for camera)* 胶卷 *jiāojuǎn*
» *(cinema)* 电影 *diànyǐng*
film star 电影明星 *diànyǐng míngxīng*
finance 金融 *jīnróng*
to find 找 *zhǎo*
fine *(penalty)* 罚款 *fákuǎn*
fire 火 *huǒ*
fire extinguisher 灭火器 *mièhuǒ qì*
firework 焰火 *yànhuǒ*
firm *(company)* 公司 *gōngsī*
» *(tough)* 强硬 *qiángyìng*
first 第一 *dìyī*
first aid 急救 *jí jiù*
fish 鱼 *yú*
to go fishing 钓鱼 *diàoyú*
fisherman 鱼民 *yúmín*

F

fishing rod 钓鱼杆 *diàoyú gǎn*
fit *(healthy)* 健康 *jiànkāng*
to fit 合适 *héshì*
fitting room 试衣室 *shìyī shì*
to fix 修 *xiū*
fizzy 带汽的 *dàiqìde*
flag 旗子 *qízi*
flash *(for camera)* 闪光灯 *shǎnguāngdēng*
flat *(apartment)* 公寓/套房 *gōngyù/tàofáng*
» *(level)* 平 *píng*
» *(battery)* 没电了 *méidiànle*
flat tyre 没气了 *méiqìle*
flavour 味道 *wèidào*
flexible 灵活 *línghuó*
flight 航班/飞机 *hángbān/fēijī*
flippers 拖鞋 *tuōxié*
flood 洪水 *hóngshuǐ*
floor *(storey)* 层 *céng*
» *(ground)* 地面 *dìmiàn*
flour 面粉 *miànfěn*
flower 花 *huā*
flu 流感 *liúgǎn*
fluent *(language)* 流利 *liúlì*
fluid 液体 *yètǐ*
fly *(insect)* 苍蝇 *cāngyíng*
to fly 飞 *fēi*
foggy 大雾 *dàwù*
foil 锡箔纸 *xībózhǐ*
folk music 民间音乐 *mínjiān yīnyuè*
to follow 紧跟, 跟着 *jǐngēn, gēnzhe*
following *(next)* 紧接着 *jǐnjiēzhe*
food 饭 *fàn*
food poisoning 食物中毒 *shíwù zhòngdú*
football 足球 *zúqiú*
for 为了 *wéile*
forbidden 不允许的 *bù yǔnxǔde*
Forbidden City 故宫/紫禁城 *gù gōng/zǐjìn chéng*
forehead 前额 *qián'é*
foreign 外国的 *wàiguóde*
foreign affairs 外交事务 *wàijiāo shìwù*
foreigner 外国人 *wàiguórén*
forest 森林 *sēnlín*
to forget 忘记 *wàngjì*
to forgive 原谅 *yuánliàng*
fork 叉子 *chāzi*
form *(document)* 表格 *biǎogé*
formal 正式 *zhèngshì*
former 从前的/前 *cóngqiánde/qián*
fortnight 两周 *liǎngzhōu*
fortunate 幸运 *xìngyùn*
fortune *(possession)* 财产 *cáichǎn*
to forward 转给 *zhuǎngěi*
forwarding address 转寄地址 *zhuǎnjì dìzhǐ*
to foster 抚养 *fǔyǎng*
foundation 基础 *jīchǔ*
fountain 泉水 *quánshuǐ*
foyer 前厅 *qiántīng*
fracture *(broken bones)* 骨折 *gǔzhé*
fragile 虚弱 *xūruò*
free *(available)* 有空 *yǒukòng*
free of charge 免费 *miǎn fèi*
free, freedom 自由 *zìyóu*
freelance 自由职业 *zìyóuzhíyè*
to freeze 冻结 *dòngjié*
freezer 冷冻柜 *lěngdòngguì*
French *(language)* 法文 *fǎwén*
» *(people)* 法国人 *fǎguórén*
frequent (adj.) 经常 *jīngcháng*
fresh 新鲜 *xīnxiān*
fridge 冰箱 *bīngxiāng*
friend 朋友 *péngyou*
friendly 友好的 *yǒuhǎode*
frightened 害怕 *hàipà*
from 从 *cóng*
front 前面 *qiánmiàn*
frost 霜 *shuāng*

frozen food 冷冻食品 *lěngdòng shípǐn*
fruit 水果 *shuǐguǒ*
frustrated 憋气/恼火 *biēqì/nǎohuǒ*
to fry 煎 *jiān*
frying pan 炒锅 *chǎo guō*
fuel 汽油/燃料 *qìyóu/ránliào*
full *(stomach)* 饱 *bǎo*
full board 吃住全包 *chīzhù quánbāo*
full up *(booked up)* 定满 *dìng mǎn*
to have fun 好好玩儿 *hǎohào wánr*
fundamental 基本的 *jīběnde*
funeral 葬礼 *zànglǐ*
funfair 儿童游乐集市 *értóng yóulè jíshì*
funny 滑稽 *huájī*
fur 毛皮 *máopí*
furniture 家具 *jiājù*
fuse 保险丝 *bǎoxiǎnsī*
future 将来 *jiānglái*

G

gallery 画廊 *huàláng*
gallon 加仑 *jiālún*
gambling 赌博 *dǔbó*
garage 修车场, 车库 *xiūchēchǎng, chēkù*
garden 花园 *huāyuán*
gardener 园丁/花匠 *yuándīng/huājiàng*
garlic 大蒜 *dàsuàn*
gas 煤气 *méiqì*
gate *(at airport)* 登机口 *dēngjīkǒu*
» *(entrance)* 大门 *dàmén*
gay 男同性恋 *nán tóngxìngliàn*
general: in general 总的来说 *zǒngde láishuō*
general *(army)* 将军 *jiāngjūn*
generous 大方/慷慨 *dàfāng/kāngkǎi*
gentle 温柔 *wēnróu*
gentleman 绅士 *shēnshì*
genuine 真的 *zhēnde*
geography 地理 *dìlǐ*
German *(people)* 德国人 *déguórén*
» *(language)* 德文 *déwén*
Germany 德国 *déguó*
to get *(something)* 拿/取 *ná/qǔ*
» *(somewhere)* 到/去 *dào/qù*
to get off *(the bus)* 下 *xià*
to get on *(the bus)* 上 *shàng*
» *(with somebody)* 相处很好 *xiāngchǔ hěn hǎo*
ghost 鬼 *guǐ*
gift 礼物 *lǐwù*
ginger 生姜 *shēngjiāng*
girl 女孩 *nǚhái*
girlfriend 女朋友 *nǚ péngyou*
give 给 *gěi*
glass *(material)* 玻璃 *bōlí*
» *(for drinks)* 玻璃杯 *bōlíbēi*
glasses 眼镜 *yǎnjìng*
global warming 全球性变暖 *quánqiúxìng biànnuǎn*
gloves 手套 *shǒutào*
glue 胶水 *jiāoshuǐ*
to go 去 *qù*
goal *(sport)* 进球 *jìnqiú*
God 上帝 *shàngdì*
goggles 游泳眼镜 *yóuyǒng yǎnjìng*
gold 金子 *jīnzi*
golden 金色/金黄色 *jīnsè/jīnhuángsè*
golden-plated 镀金 *dù jīn*
golf 高儿夫 *gāo'érfū*
» golf clubs 高尔夫球棍 *gāo'érfū qiúgùn*
» golf course 高尔夫球场 *gāo'érfū qiúchǎng*
good 好 *hǎo*
» good evening 晚上好 *wǎnshàng hǎo*
» good morning 早上好 *zǎoshàng hǎo*

» **good night** 晚安 *wǎn'ān*
goodbye 再见 *zàijiàn*
good-looking 好看 *hǎokàn*
goods 货物 *huòwù*
gorgeous 非常好/妙极了 *fēicháng hǎo/miàojíle*
to gossip 闲聊/说闲话 *xiánliáo/shuō xiánhuà*
to govern 管理 *guǎnlǐ*
government 政府 *zhèngfǔ*
gradual 逐渐 *zhújiàn*
graduate *(student)* 毕业生, 研究生 *bìyèshēng, yánjiùshēng*
to graduate 毕业 *bìyè*
grammar 语法 *yǔfǎ*
gramme 克 *kè*
grand 宏伟 *hóngwěi*
granddaughter 孙女, 外孙女 *sūnnǚ, wài sūnnǚ*
grandfather 爷爷, 外公 *yéye, wài gōng*
grandmother 奶奶, 外婆 *nǎinai, wàipó*
grandparents 祖父母, 外祖父母 *zǔfùmǔ, wài zǔfùmǔ*
grandson 孙子, 外孙 *sūnzi, wàisūn*
grant *(fund)* 补助金 *bǔzhùjīn*
grass 草 *cǎo*
grateful 感激 *gǎnjī*
grave *(cemetery)* 坟墓 *fénmù*
greasy 油腻 *yóunì*
great 伟大 *wěidà*
Great Wall 长城 *cháng chéng*
greedy 贪婪 *tānlán*
green 绿色 *lǜsè*
greengrocer's 蔬菜水果店 *shūcài shuǐguǒ diàn*
grey 灰色 *huīsè*
grilled 烧烤的 *shāokǎode*
grocer's 食品店 *shípǐn diàn*
ground 地 *dì*
ground floor 一层 *yī céng*
group 小组/团 *xiǎo zǔ/tuán*
to grow *(plant)* 种 *zhǒng*
to grow up 长大 *zhǎngdà*
to guarantee 保证 *bǎozhèng*
guest 客人 *kèrén*
guesthouse 宾馆 *bīnguǎn*
guide: tourist guide 导游 *dǎoyóu*
to guide 引导/带领 *yǐndǎo/dàilǐng*
guidebook 导游书 *dǎoyóu shū*
guilty 内疚 *nèijiù*
guitar 吉它 *jítā*
gun 枪 *qiāng*
gymnasium 健身房, 体操馆 *jiànshēnfáng, tǐcāoguǎn*
gymnastics 体操 *tǐcāo*

H

hair 头发 *tóufà*
hairbrush 梳子 *shūzi*
haircut 剪头发 *jiǎn tóufà*
hairdresser's 发廊 *fàláng*
hair dryer 吹风机 *chuī fēngjī*
hairspray 喷发定型剂 *pēnfà dìngxíngjì*
half (n) 半 *bàn*
hamburger 汉堡包 *hànbǎobāo*
hammer 锤子 *chuízi*
hand luggage 手提行李 *shǒutí hánglǐ*
handbag 手提包 *shǒutíbāo*
handicapped 残疾人 *cánjírén*
handkerchief 手绢 *shǒujuàn*
handle 把/扶手 *bà/fúshǒu*
handmade 手工做的 *shǒugōng zuòde*
to hang up 挂起来 *guà qǐlái*
hangover 宿醉/酒后头痛等 *sù zuì/jiǔhòu tóutòng děng*
to happen 发生 *fāshēng*
happy 高兴 *gāoxìng*
harbour 港湾 *gǎngwān*

hard *(not soft)* 硬 *yìng*
» *(difficult)* 难 *nán*
hard drive 硬盘 *yìng pán*
hat 帽子 *màozi*
hate 恨 *hèn*
have 有 *yǒu*
hay fever 花粉病 *huāfěn bìng*
he 他 *tā*
headache 头疼 *tóuténg*
headphones 耳机 *ěrjī*
headquarters 总部 *zǒngbù*
health 身体 *shēntǐ*
health foods 健康食品 *jiànkāng shípǐn*
healthy 健康 *jiànkāng*
to hear 听到 *tīng dào*
hearing aid 助听器 *zhùtīng qì*
heart 心脏 *xīnzàng*
heart attack 心肌梗塞 *xīnjī gěngsè*
heat 热气 *rèqì*
heating 暖气 *nuǎnqì*
heaven 天堂 *tiāntáng*
heavy 重 *zhòng*
heel 脚后跟 *jiǎohòugēn*
height *(person)* 身高 *shēngāo*
» *(object)* 高度 *gāodù*
helicopter 直升飞机 *zhíshēng fēijī*
hell 地狱 *dìyù*
hello 你好 *nǐ hǎo*
helmet 头盔 *tóukuī*
to help 帮助 *bāngzhù*
Help! 救命 *jiùmìng*
hepatitis 肝炎 *gānyán*
her *(possessive)* 她的 *tāde*
» *(in object position)* 她 *tā*
herb 草药 *cǎoyào*
herbal tea 香草茶 *xiāngcǎo chá*
here 这儿 *zhèr*
hers 她的 *tāde*
hiccup 打嗝 *dǎgé*
high 高 *gāo*
high chair 幼儿高椅子 *yòu'ér gāo yǐzi*
high school 中学 *zhōng xué*
to hijack 劫持 *jiéchí*
him 他 *tā*
to hire *(employ)* 雇用 *gùyòng*
» *(rent)* 租 *zū*
his 他的 *tāde*
history 历史 *lìshǐ*
to hitchhike 搭车 *dāchē*
HIV 艾滋病毒 *àizī bìngdú*
» **HIV positive** 艾滋病毒阳性 *àizī bìngdú yángxìng*
hobby 爱好 *àihào*
to hold *(sth.)* 拿着 *názhe*
» *(a meeting)* 开 *kāi*
holiday 度假/假期 *dùjià/jiàqī*
holy 神圣的 *shénshèngde*
home 家 *jiā*
to be homesick 想家 *xiǎng jiā*
homosexual 同性恋 *tóngxìngliàn*
honest 正直的, 说实话 *zhèngzhíde, shuō shíhuà*
honeymoon 蜜月 *mìyuè*
Hong Kong 香港 *xiāng gǎng*
to hope 希望 *xīwàng*
horrible 糟透了 *zāotòule*
horse 马 *mǎ*
horse racing 赛马 *sài mǎ*
hospital 医院 *yīyuàn*
hospitality 好客 *hàokè*
host 主人 *zhǔrén*
hostess 女主人 *nǚ zhǔrén*
hot *(spicy)* 辣 *là*
» *(for food and drinks)* 烫 *tàng*
» *(weather)* 热 *rè*
hot and sour 酸辣 *suān là*
hotel 饭店/宾馆 *fàndiàn/bīnguǎn*
hour 小时 *xiǎoshí*
house 房子 *fángzi*
housewife 家庭主妇 *jiātíng zhǔfù*
housework 家务事 *jiāwùshì*

how 怎么 zěnme
how are things? 怎么样 zěn me yàng
how are you? 你好吗 nǐ hǎo ma
how far? 多远 duō yuǎn
how long? 多久 duō jiǔ
how many? (small number) 几 jǐ
» (large number) 多少 duō shǎo
how much? 多少钱 duōshǎo qián
how old? 多大了 duō dà le
humid 潮湿 cháoshī
humour 幽默 yōumò
hundred 百 bǎi
to be hungry 饿 è
to be in a hurry 有急事 yǒu jí shì
to hurry up 赶快 gǎn kuài
to hurt 疼 téng
to be hurt (emotion) 伤心 shāng xīn
husband 丈夫/先生 zhàngfu/xiānshēng

I

I 我 wǒ
ice 冰 bīng
icy 结冰了 jiébīngle
idea 主意/想法 zhǔyì/xiǎngfǎ
if 如果 rúguǒ
ill 病了 bìngle
illness 疾病 jíbìng
to imagine 想象 xiǎngxiàng
immediately 马上/立即 mǎshàng/lìjí
impatient 不耐心 búnàixīn
to import 进口 jìnkǒu
important 重要 zhòngyào
impossible 不可能 bùkěnéng
in 在 zài
to include, included 包括 bāokuò
income 收入 shōurù
indeed 确实 quèshí
independent 独立 dúlì
indigestion 不消化 bùxiāohuà
indoors 室内 shìnèi
industry 工业 gōngyè
inexpensive 便宜 piányí
in fact 实际上 shíjì shàng
infection 感染/发炎 gǎnrǎn/fāyán
inflammation 红肿 hóngzhǒng
influenza 流感 liúgǎn
informal 不正式，随便 búzhèngshì, suíbiàn
information 信息 xìnxí
information desk 问询处 wènxún chù
injection 打针 dǎzhēn
to injure 受伤 shòushāng
ink 墨水 mòshuǐ
innocent (naive) 天真 tiānzhēn
» (not guilty) 无辜 wúgū
insect 昆虫 kūnchóng
insect bite 虫子咬的 chóngzi yǎode
insect repellent 驱虫剂 qūchóng jì
inside 在...里面 zài...lǐmiàn
to insist 坚持 jiānchí
inspector 检察官 jiǎncháguān
instant coffee 速溶咖啡 sùróng kāfēi
instead of 而不是，替代 ér búshì, tìdài
instructor 教官 jiàoguān
to insult 侮辱 wǔrǔ
insurance 保险 bǎoxiǎn
intelligent 聪明 cōngmíng
interest (bank) 利息 lìxí
interested 感兴趣 gǎnxìngqù
interesting 有意思 yǒuyìsī
international 国际 guójì
Internet 互联网 hùliánwǎng
Internet café 网吧 wǎng bā
Internet connection 联网 lián wǎng
to interpret, interpreter 翻译 fānyì
interval 间歇 jiānxiē
to interview 面试 miànshì
to introduce 介绍 jièshào
invitation 邀请 yāoqǐng

to invite 邀请/请 *yāoqǐng/qǐng*
iPod IP四 *IP sì*
Ireland 爱尔兰 *ài'ěrlán*
Irish 爱尔兰人 *ài'ěrlánrén*
iron 铁 *tiě*
is 是 *shì*
Islam 伊斯兰 *yīsīlán*
Islamic 伊斯兰教的 *yīsīlán jiàode*
island 岛 *dǎo*
it 它 *tā*
itchy 痒 *yǎng*
itinerary 旅行日程 *lǚxíng rìchéng*
ivory 象牙 *xiàngyá*

J

jacket 上衣 *shàngyī*
jade 玉 *yù*
jam 果酱 *guǒjiàng*
Japan 日本 *rìběn*
Japanese *(language)* 日文 *rìwén*
» *(people)* 日本人 *rìběnrén*
jasmine tea 茉莉花茶 *mòlìhuā chá*
jazz 爵士音乐 *juéshì yīnyuè*
jeans 牛仔裤 *niúzǎi kù*
jellyfish 海蜇 *hǎizhé*
Jesus Christ 耶稣基督 *yēsū jīdū*
jewel 首饰 *shǒushì*
jeweller's 珠宝店 *zhūbǎo diàn*
Jewish 犹太人 *yóutàirén*
job 工作 *gōngzuò*
jog, jogging 跑步 *pǎobù*
to join 参加 *cānjiā*
joke 笑话 *xiàohuà*
journalist 记者 *jìzhě*
journey 旅行, 路途 *lǚxíng, lùtú*
to judge, judgement 判断 *pànduàn*
juice 汁/水 *zhī/shuǐ*
to jump 跳 *tiào*
jumper 毛衣 *máoyī*

K

to keep 留下 *liúxià*
kettle 水壶 *shuǐhú*
key 钥匙 *yàoshi*
to kill 杀 *shā*
kilogramme 公斤 *gōngjīn*
kilometre 公里 *gōnglǐ*
kind *(type)* 种类 *zhǒnglèi*
» *(good-hearted)* 好心 *hǎoxīn*
king 国王 *guówáng*
to kiss 吻/亲吻 *wěn/qīnwěn*
kitchen 厨房 *chúfáng*
knickers 内裤 *nèikù*
knife 刀 *dāo*
knitting 编织 *biānzhī*
knitting needle 毛衣针 *máoyī zhēn*
to knock 敲 *qiāo*
knot 结 *jié*
to know 知道 *zhīdào*
knowledge 知识 *zhīshi*
Korea 朝鲜 *cháoxiān*
» South Korea 韩国 *hánguó*

L

label 标签 *biāoqiān*
lace 花边 *huābiān*
laces *(for shoes)* 鞋带 *xiédài*
ladies 女厕所 *nǚcèsuǒ*
lady 女士 *nǚshì*
lager 清啤酒 *qīng píjiǔ*
lake 湖 *hú*
lamb 羊肉 *yángròu*
lamp 灯 *dēng*
lamp post 路灯柱 *lù dēngzhǔ*
land 土地 *tǔdì*
language 语言 *yǔyán*
laptop 手提电脑 *shǒutí diànnǎo*
large 大 *dà*
late 晚 *wǎn*
» be late 迟到 *chídào*
lately 最近 *zuìjìn*

later 后来 *hòulái*
laugh 笑 *xiào*
laundry 洗衣房 *xǐyīfáng*
lavatory 厕所 *cèsuǒ*
law 法律 *fǎlǜ*
lawyer 律师 *lǜshī*
laxative 泻药 *xièyào*
lazy 懒 *lǎn*
lead *(electrical)* 电线 *diànxiàn*
leaf 树叶 *shùyè*
leaflet 传单 *chuándān*
to leak *(water)* 漏 *lòu*
to lean 靠 *kào*
to learn 学 *xué*
leather 皮革 *pígé*
to leave 离开/走 *líkāi/zǒu*
lecturer 讲师 *jiǎngshī*
left 左 *zuǒ*
left-luggage 行李寄存处 *xínglǐ jìcúnchǔ*
legal 合法 *héfǎ*
lemon 柠檬 *níngméng*
lemonade 柠檬汁 *níngméngzhī*
to lend 借 *jiè*
length 长度/长短 *chángdù/chángduǎn*
lens *(camera)* 镜头 *jìngtóu*
» *(contact lenses)* 镜片 *jìngpiàn*
lesbian 女同性恋者 *nǚ tóngxìngliàn zhě*
less 少 *shǎo*
lesson 课 *kè*
letter 信 *xìn*
level 水平 *shuǐpíng*
library 图书馆 *túshūguǎn*
to lie *(untruth)* 说谎 *shuōhuǎng*
to lie down 躺下 *tǎng xià*
lifeboat 救生艇 *jiùshēngtǐng*
lifeguard 救生员 *jiùshēngyuán*
lifejacket 救生衣 *jiùshēngyī*
lift 电梯 *diàntī*

light *(not heavy)* 轻 *qīng*
» *(colour)* 浅 *qiǎn*
to light 点火 *diǎnhuǒ*
light bulb 灯泡 *dēng pào*
lightening 闪电 *shǎndiàn*
lighter *(cigarette)* 打火机 *dǎhuǒjī*
like *(similar)* 像 *xiàng*
to like 喜欢 *xǐhuān*
likely 可能 *kěnéng*
limited 有限的 *yǒuxiànde*
limited company 有限公司 *yǒuxiàn gōngsī*
linen *(bed)* 床单 *chuángdān*
» *(fabric)* 亚麻 *yàmá*
linguist 语言学家 *yǔyánxuéjiā*
lion 狮子 *shīzi*
lip 嘴唇 *zuǐchún*
lipstick 口红 *kǒuhóng*
liqueur 酒 *jiǔ*
liquid 液体 *yètǐ*
liquor 酒 *jiǔ*
list 目录，单子 *mùlù, dānzi*
to listen 听 *tīng*
litre 升 *shēng*
litter *(rubbish)* 废物 *fèiwù*
little 小 *xiǎo*
» a little 一点 *yīdiǎn*
to live 住 *zhù*
loan 贷款 *dàikuǎn*
lobby 前堂大厅 *qiántáng dàtīng*
lobster 龙虾 *lóngxiā*
local 当地 *dāngdì*
to lock 锁 *suǒ*
locker 锁柜 *suǒguì*
lonely 孤单 *gūdān*
long *(length)* 长 *cháng*
» *(time)* 久 *jiǔ*
long distance 长途 *chángtú*
to look 看 *kàn*
to look for 找 *zhǎo*
loose 松 *sōng*

lorry 卡车 *kǎchē*
to lose 丢失 *diūshī*
lost property 失物 *shī wù*
lot: a lot 很多 *hěn duō*
loud 大声地, 吵闹 *dàshēngdì, chǎonào*
to love 爱 *ài*
lovely 可爱, 真好 *kě'ài, zhēnhǎo*
low-fat 低脂肪 *dī zhīfáng*
lower 下 *xià*
luck 运气 *yùnqì*
lucky 运气好 *yùnqìhǎo*
luggage 行李 *xínglǐ*
lunch 午饭/中饭 *wǔfàn/zhōngfàn*
luxury 豪华 *háohuá*
lychee 荔枝 *lìzhī*

M

machine 机器 *jīqì*
mad 疯 *fēng*
madam 女士 *nǚshì*
magazine 杂志 *zázhì*
magnificent 好极了 *hǎojíle*
maid 女服务生, 女佣人 *nǚ fúwùshēng, nǚ yòngrén*
mail 邮件/信件 *yóujiàn/xìnjiàn*
mailbox 信箱 *xìnxiāng*
main 主要 *zhǔyào*
to make 做 *zuò*
» a phone call 打电话 *dǎ diànhuà*
» a reservation 预约 *yù yuē*
» a speech 讲话 *jiǎng huà*
make-up 化妆品 *huàzhuāng pǐn*
male 男的 *nánde*
man 男人 *nánrén*
to manage 管理 *guǎnlǐ*
manager *(company)* 经理 *jīnglǐ*
» *(factory)* 厂长 *chǎngzhǎng*
managing director 总经理 *zǒng jīnglǐ*
Mandarin 普通话 *pǔtōnghuà*
manual worker 工人 *gōngrén*
many 很多 *hěnduō*
map 地图 *dìtú*
marble 大理石 *dàlǐshí*
margarine 植物黄油 *zhíwù huángyóu*
market 自由市场 *zìyóu shìchǎng*
married 结婚了/已婚 *jiéhūnle/yǐhūn*
martial art 武术 *wǔ shù*
masculine 男性化 *nánxìnghuà*
mask 面具 *miànjù*
match *(competition)* 比赛 *bǐsài*
matches 火柴 *huǒchái*
material *(fabric)* 布料 *bùliào*
mathematics 数学 *shùxué*
matter 事 *shì*
» it doesn't matter 没关系 *méi guānxì*
mattress 垫子 *diànzi*
mature 成熟 *chéngshóu*
maybe 也许 *yěxǔ*
me 我 *wǒ*
meal 饭 *fàn*
meaning 意思 *yìsi*
meanwhile 同时 *tóngshí*
measles 麻疹 *mázhěn*
to measure 衡量/量 *héng liàng/liàng*
measurement *(clothes)* 尺寸 *chǐcùn*
meat 肉 *ròu*
mechanic 技师 *jìshī*
medical 医学的 *yīxuéde*
medicine 药 *yào*
Mediterranean 地中海 *dìzhōnghǎi*
medium 中等 *zhōngděng*
medium-sized 中号 *zhōnghào*
to meet 见面 *jiànmiàn*
» *(somebody)* 见/见到 *jiàn/jiàndào*
meeting 会议 *huìyì*
melon 甜瓜 *tiánguā*
member 成员 *chéngyuán*
memory 记忆 *jìyì*
memory stick 记忆棒 *jìyì bàng*
men 男的/男人们 *nánde/nánrénmen*

to mend *(repair)* 修 *xiū*
men's toilet 男厕所 *nán cèsuǒ*
menu 菜单 *càidān*
» **set menu** 套餐 *tàocān*
message 口信 *kǒuxìn*
metal 金属 *jīnshǔ*
meter *(for taxi)* 计程器 *jìchéngqì*
metre 米 *mǐ*
microwave oven 微波炉 *wéibō lú*
midday 中午 *zhōngwǔ*
middle *(size)* 中等 *zhōngděng*
» *(location)* 中间 *zhōngjiān*
middle-aged 中年 *zhōng nián*
middle-class 中产阶级 *zhōngchǎn jiējí*
midnight 半夜 *bànyè*
mid-range hotel 中等旅馆 *zhōng děng lǚguǎn*
might 可能/也许 *kěnéng/yěxǔ*
mild *(food)* 清淡 *qīngdàn*
» *(weather)* 暖和 *nuǎnhé*
mile 英里 *yīnglǐ*
military 军事 *jūnshì*
milk 牛奶 *niúnǎi*
mind: I don't mind 我不介意 *wǒ bú jièyì*
mine *(possessive)* 我的 *wǒde*
mineral water 矿泉水 *kuàngquán shuǐ*
mini-bus 小公共汽车/小面包车 *xiǎo gōnggòng qìchē /xiǎo miànbāochē*
minister 部长 *bùzhǎng*
minute *(time)* 分 *fēn*
minutes *(of a meeting)* 会议记录 *huìyì jìlù*
mirror 镜子 *jìngzi*
Miss 小姐 *xiǎojiě*
to miss *(bus, train)* 误了/没赶上 *wù le/méi gǎnshàng*
» *(someone)* 想 *xiǎng*
mistake 错误 *cuòwù*
misunderstanding 误解 *wùjiě*
mixed 混杂 *hùnzá*
mixture 混合物 *hùnhéwù*
mobile *(phone)* 手机 *shǒujī*
modem 调制解调器 *tiáozhì jiětiàoqì*
modern 现代 *xiàndài*
moisturiser 护肤霜 *hùfūshuāng*
moment: at the moment 目前 *mùqián*
monastery 寺庙 *sìmiào*
money 钱 *qián*
Mongolia 蒙古 *ménggǔ*
Mongolian hot pot 火锅 *huǒ guō*
monosodium glutamate 味精 *wèi jīng*
month 月 *yuè*
monthly 每月的 *měiyuède*
monthly pass 月票 *yuè piào*
monument 纪念碑 *jìniànbēi*
moon 月亮 *yuèliàng*
moon cake 月饼 *yuè bǐng*
more 多一点 *duōyīdiǎn*
morning 早上/上午 *zǎoshàng/ shàngwǔ*
mortgage 抵押 *dǐyā*
mosque 清真寺 *qīngzhēnsì*
mosquito 蚊子 *wénzi*
mosquito net 蚊帐 *wén zhàng*
mother 母亲 *mǔqīn*
motorbike 摩托车 *mótuōchē*
motorboat 摩托艇 *mótuōtǐng*
motor racing 赛车 *sài chē*
motorway 高速公路 *gāosù gōnglù*
mountain 山 *shān*
mountaineering 登山运动 *dēngshān yùndòng*
moustache 小胡子 *xiǎo húzi*
mouth 嘴, 口 *zuǐ, kǒu*
movie 电影 *diànyǐng*
Mr. 先生 *xiānsheng*
Mrs. 太太/夫人 *tàitài/fūrén*

much 多 duō
mug 杯子 bēizi
mum 妈, 娘 mā, niáng
to murder 谋杀 móushā
muscle 肌肉 jīròu
museum 博物馆 bówùguǎn
mushroom 蘑菇 mógū
music 音乐 yīnyuè
musical 会音乐的 huìyīnyuè de
musician 音乐家 yīnyuè jiā
Muslim 穆斯林 mùsīlín
must 必须 bìxū
my 我的 wǒde
myself 我自己 wǒ zìjǐ

N

nail (finger, toe) 指甲 zhǐjia
to nail 钉 dìng
nail clippers 指甲刀 zhǐjia dāo
nail polish 指甲油 zhǐjia yóu
naked 裸体 luǒtǐ
name 名字 míngzì
nap 午觉 wǔjiào
napkin (for dining) 餐巾 cānjīn
nappy: disposable 一次性尿布 yīcìxìng niàobù
narrow 窄 zhǎi
national 全国的 quánguóde
nationality 国籍 guójí
natural 自然 zìrán
naughty 调皮 tiáopí
nausea 恶心 ěxīn
navy 海军 hǎijūn
near, nearby 附近 fùjìn
nearest 最近的 zuìjìnde
nearly 差点儿 chādiǎnr
necessary 必要 bìyào
necklace 项链 xiàngliàn
to need 需要 xūyào
needle 针 zhēn
negative (not positive) 消极/不好的 xiāojí/bùhǎode
» (photo) 底片 dǐpiàn
neighbour 邻居 línjū
neither...nor... 不是...也不是... búshì... yěbúshì...
nervous 紧张 jǐnzhāng
never 从来不 cóngláibù
new 新 xīn
news 新闻 xīnwén
newspaper 报纸 bàozhǐ
New Year 新年 xīn nián
» Chinese New Year 春节 chūn jié
New Zealand 新西兰 xīn xīlán
next 下个 xiàge
next to 旁边 pángbiān
nice 好 hǎo
night 夜里 yèlǐ
nightclub 夜总会 yèzǒnghuì
nightdress 睡衣 shuìyī
no 不 bù
nobody 没人 méirén
no entry 禁止入内/不准入内 jìnzhǐ rùnèi/bùzhǔn rùnèi
noisy 吵闹 chǎonào
non-alcoholic 不含酒精 bùhán jiǔjīng
none 都不是 dōubúshì
nonsense 胡说 húshuō
non-smoking 不许吸烟 bùxǔ xīyān
no smoking 请勿吸烟 qǐngwù xīyān
normal 正常 zhèngcháng
normally 通常 tōngcháng
north 北 běi
northeast 东北 dōngběi
northwest 西北 xīběi
nose 鼻子 bízi
nosebleed 流鼻血 liú bíxiě
not at all 哪里 nǎ lǐ
note (money) 纸币 zhǐbì
to note 注意 zhùyì
nothing 没什么 méishénme

now 现在 *xiànzài*
number 号码/号 *hàomǎ; hào*
nurse 护士 *hùshì*
nursery 幼儿园 *yòuéryuán*
nut 果仁 *guǒrén*
nylon 尼龙 *nílóng*

O

obvious 明显 *míngxiǎn*
occasionally 偶尔 *ǒu'ěr*
occupied 有人 *yǒurén*
o'clock 点/点钟 *diǎn/diǎnzhōng*
odd *(strange)* 奇怪 *qíguài*
offended 生气了 *shēngqìle*
offer *(price)* 要价 *yàojià*
to offer 给 *gěi*
office *(room)* 办公室 *bàngōngshì*
» *(branch)* 办事处 *bànshìchù*
officer 官员 *guānyuán*
official 官方的 *guānfāngde*
often 常常 *chángcháng*
oil 油 *yóu*
okay 好的/行 *hǎode/xíng*
old 老 *lǎo*
old-fashioned 老式/过时 *lǎo shì/guò shí*
Olympic Games 奥林匹克运动会 *àolínpǐkè yùndòng huì*
Olympic village 奥林匹克村 *àolínpǐkè cūn*
on 在...上 *zài...shàng*
once *(one time)* 一次 *yīcì*
» *(formerly)* 曾经 *céngjīng*
only 只有 *zhīyǒu*
to open 打开 *dǎkāi*
opera 歌剧 *gējù*
» Peking Opera 京剧 *jīng jù*
to operate *(medical)* 开刀 *kāidāo*
operation *(medical)* 手术 *shǒushù*
opinion 意见 *yìjiàn*
opportunity 机会 *jīhuì*
opposite 对面 *duìmiàn*
optician 眼镜店 *yǎnjìng diàn*
optimistic 乐观 *lèguān*
or *(in statement)* 或者 *huòzhě*
» *(in question)* 还是 *háishì*
orange 橙子/柑子 *chéngzi/gānzi*
orange juice 橘子水/橙汁 *júzi shuǐ/chéng zhī*
to order *(food)* 点菜 *diǎn cài*
ordinary 普通 *pǔtōng*
organization 机关/机构 *jīguān/jīgòu*
to organize 组织 *zǔzhī*
original *(earliest)* 原来的 *yuánláide*
» *(new)* 新颖的 *xīnyǐngde*
other 别的 *biéde*
our, ours 我们的 *wǒmende*
outdoors 露天 *lùtiān*
outside 外面 *wàimiàn*
oven 烤箱 *kǎoxiāng*
over *(more than)* 多 *duō*
» *(on top)* 在...上 *zài...shàng*
overcast 多云 *duōyún*
overcharge 多收钱 *duō shōuqián*
overweight 超重 *chāozhòng*
to owe 欠 *qiàn*
owner 主人 *zhǔrén*
oyster sauce 蚝油 *háo yóu*
ozone layer 臭氧层 *chòuyǎng céng*

P

pack, packet 包 *bāo*
package 包装 *bāozhuāng*
package tour 包团假期 *bāotuán jiàqī*
page 页 *yè*
pagoda 塔 *tǎ*
pain, painful 疼 *téng*
painkiller 止疼药 *zhǐténg yào*
to paint *(a house)* 漆 *qī*
» *(painting)* 画 *huà*
painter 画家 *huàjiā*
painting 画 *huà*

pair 对 duì
pajamas 睡衣 shuìyī
palace 宫殿 gōngdiàn
pale 苍白 cāngbái
pancake 饼 bǐng
panda 熊猫 xióngmāo
panic 慌张 huāngzhāng
pants 短裤, 裤子 duǎnkù, kùzi
paper 纸 zhǐ
paralysed 瘫痪了 tānhuànle
parcel 包裹 bāoguǒ
pardon 对不起 duìbùqǐ
parents 父母 fùmǔ
park 公园 gōngyuán
to park 停车 tíngchē
parking: no parking 不许停车 bùxǔ tíngchē
» car park 停车场 tíngchē cháng
parliament 议会 yìhuì
part *(for a car)* 零件 língjiàn
» *(proportion)* 部分 bùfèn
particular: in particular 特别是 tèbiéshì
partner *(business)* 伙伴 huǒbàn
» *(personal)* 爱人 àirén
party *(political)* 党 dǎng
» *(group)* 团体 tuántǐ
» *(get-together)* 聚会 jùhuì
to pass *(a test)* 及格 jígé
passenger 乘客/旅客 chéngkè/ lǚkè
passion 热情 rèqíng
passport 护照 hùzhào
passport control 护照检查 hùzhào jiǎnchá
password 密码 mìmǎ
past 过去/从前 guòqù/ cóngqián
pasta 意大利面片 yìdàlì miànpiàn
pastry 面团儿 miàntuánr
path 小路 xiǎolù
patience, patient 耐心 nàixīn
patient *(sick person)* 病人 bìngrén
pattern 图案/格式 tú'àn/géshì
pavement 人行道 rénxíngdào
to pay 付/支付 fù/zhīfù
peace 和平 hépíng
peach 桃子 táozi
pear 梨子 lízi
pearl 珍珠 zhēnzhū
peanut 花生 huāshēng
pedestrian crossing 人行横道 rénxíng héngdào
to peel 剥 bō
peg 衣夹子 yījiázi
pen 笔 bǐ
pencil 铅笔 qiānbǐ
penfriend 笔友 bǐyǒu
penicillin 青霉素 qīngméisù
penis 生殖器 shēngzhíqì
pension 养老金 yǎnglǎojīn
pensioner 领养老金的人 lǐng yǎnglǎojīnde rén
people 人 rén
People's Daily 人民日报 rénmín rìbào
P. R. China 中华人民共和国 zhōnghuá rénmín gònghé guó
perfect 完美/完好 wánměi/wánhǎo
perfume 香水 xiāngshuǐ
perhaps 也许 yěxǔ
period *(of time)* 时期 shíqī
» *(menstrual)* 月经 yuèjīng
permission 允许/同意 yǔnxǔ/tóngyì
person 人 rén
personal 个人的 gèrénde
personnel 人事 rénshì
pessimistic 悲观 bēiguān
petrol 汽油 qìyóu
petrol station 加油站 jiāyóu zhàn
pharmacy 药店 yàodiàn
philosophy 哲学 zhéxué
photocopy 复印件 fùyìn jiān
photograph 照片 zhàopiàn
photographer 摄影师 shèyǐngshī

phrase book 小词典, 手册 *xiǎo cídiǎn, shǒu cè*
physics 物理 *wùlǐ*
piano 钢琴 *gāngqín*
to **pick** *(choose)* 挑 *tiǎo*
pickpocket 小偷/扒手 *xiǎotōu/ bāshǒu*
picnic 野餐 *yěcān*
picture *(film)* 电影 *diànyǐng*
» *(painting)* 画 *huà*
» *(photo)* 照片 *zhàopiàn*
piece 块 *kuài*
pier 码头 *mǎtóu*
pig 猪 *zhū*
pigeon 鸽子 *gēzi*
pill 药丸 *yàowán*
pillow 枕头 *zhěntóu*
pilot 飞行员 *fēixíngyuán*
pin 别针 *biézhēn*
pineapple 菠萝 *bōluó*
pink 粉色 *fěnsè*
pipe 管子 *guǎnzi*
pity: what a pity! 真可惜 *zhēn kěxí*
pizza 比萨 *bǐsà*
place 地方 *dìfāng*
to **plan** 计划 *jìhuà*
plane 飞机 *fēijī*
plant 植物 *zhíwù*
plasters 创可贴 *chuàngkětiē*
plastic 塑料 *sùliào*
plate 盘子 *pánzi*
platform 站台 *zhàntái*
play 话剧 *huàjù*
to **play** 玩儿 *wánr*
please 请 *qǐng*
pleased 高兴 *gāoxìng*
plenty 很多 *hěnduō*
plug *(bath)* 塞子 *sāizi*
» *(electrical)* 插头 *chātóu*
plum 李子 *lǐzi*
plumber 水暖工 *shuǐnuǎngōng*

p.m. 下午 *xiàwǔ*
pneumonia 肺炎 *fèiyán*
pocket 口袋 *kǒudài*
point 点 *diǎn*
to **point** 指出 *zhǐchū*
poisonous 有毒 *yǒudú*
police, policeman 警察 *jǐngchá*
police station 警察局/公安局 *jǐngchá jú/gōngān jú*
polish: shoe polish 鞋油 *xié yóu*
polite 有礼貌 *yǒulǐmào*
political 政治的 *zhèngzhìde*
politician 政治家 *zhèngzhìjiā*
politics 政治 *zhèngzhì*
pollution 污染 *wūrǎn*
pond 池塘 *chítáng*
pool *(swimming)* 游泳池 *yóuyǒng chí*
poor 穷 *qióng*
pop music 流行音乐 *liúxíng yīnyuè*
Pope 大主教 *dàzhǔjiào*
popular 受欢迎 *shòu huānyíng*
population 人口 *rénkǒu*
pork 猪肉 *zhūròu*
portable 手提式 *shǒutíshì*
porter 服务员 *fúwùyuán*
positive *(attitude)* 积极 *jījí*
possible, possibly 可能 *kěnéng*
as…as possible 尽可能… *jìn kěnéng…*
to **post** 寄 *jì*
postbox 信箱 *xìnxiāng*
postcard 明信片 *míngxìnpiàn*
postcode 邮编 *yóubiān*
poster 宣传画 *xuānchuán huà*
post office 邮局 *yóujú*
to **postpone** 推迟/延期 *tuīchí/ yánqī*
potato 土豆 *tǔdòu*
pottery 陶器 *táoqì*
potty 尿盆 *niàopén*
pound *(sterling)* 镑 *bàng*
to **pour** 倒 *dào*
powder 粉 *fěn*

powered milk 奶粉 *nǎi fěn*
power *(electricity)* 供电 *gōngdiàn*
» *(control)* 权力 *quánlì*
» **power cut** 停电 *tíng diàn*
pram 婴儿车 *yīng'ér chē*
prawn 大虾 *dàxiā*
to prefer 更喜欢 *gèng xǐhuān*
pregnant 怀孕 *huáiyùn*
to prepare 准备 *zhǔnbèi*
prescription 药方 *yàofāng*
present *(gift)* 礼物 *lǐwù*
press *(newspaper)* 报界 *bàojiè*
to press 压 *yā*
pretty 好看 *hǎokàn*
price 价格 *jiàgé*
priest 牧师 *mùshī*
prime minister 首相 *shǒu xiàng*
prince 王子 *wángzi*
princess 公主 *gōngzhǔ*
to print 印 *yìn*
prison 监狱 *jiānyù*
private 私人 *sīrén*
prize 奖品 *jiǎngpǐn*
probably 有可能 *yǒu kěnéng*
problem 问题 *wèntí*
profession 职业 *zhíyè*
profit 利润 *lìrùn*
programme 节目 *jiémù*
prohibited 受限制 *shòuxiànzhì*
to promise 保证 *bǎozhèng*
to pronounce 念 *niàn*
pronunciation 发音 *fāyīn*
property 房屋 *fángwū*
prostitute 妓女 *jìnǚ*
to protect 保护 *bǎohù*
proud 骄傲 *jiāoào*
public 公共 *gōnggòng*
public phone 公共电话 *gōnggòng diànhuà*
to pull 拉 *lā*
pullover 套头毛衣 *tàotóu máoyī*
puncture 轮胎刺孔 *lúntāi cìkǒng*
pure 纯 *chún*
purple 紫色 *zǐsè*
purse 钱包 *qiánbāo*
to push 推 *tuī*
push-chair 推车 *tuīchē*
to put 放 *fàng*
to put on 穿 *chuān*
pyjamas 睡衣 *shuìyī*

Q

quality 质量 *zhìliàng*
quay 码头 *mǎtóu*
queen 女王 *nǚwáng*
question 问题 *wèntí*
queue 队 *duì*
quick, quickly 快 *kuài*
quiet 安静 *ānjìng*
quite 相当/比较 *xiāngdāng/bǐjiào*

R

rabbi 犹太教的大师 *yóutàijiào de dàshī*
rabbit 兔子 *tùzi*
race *(sport)* 比赛 *bǐsài*
radio 收音机 *shōuyīnjī*
radioactive 放射性的 *fàngshè xìngde*
radio station 电台 *diàn tái*
railway station 火车站 *huǒchē zhàn*
rain 雨 *yǔ*
to rain 下雨 *xiàyǔ*
to rape 强奸 *qiángjiān*
rare 稀有 *xīyǒu*
rash 皮疹 *pízhěn*
rat 老鼠 *lǎoshǔ*
rate *(exchange rate)* 兑换率 *duìhuàn lǜ*
rather *(quite)* 相当地 *xiāngdāngdī*
raw *(meat)* 生 *shēng*
razor 剃胡刀/剃须刀 *tìhúdāo/tìxūdāo*

razor blade 刀片 *dāo piàn*
to **reach** 够 *gòu*
to **read** 读/念 *dú/niàn*
ready 准备好了 *zhǔnbèi hǎole*
real, really 真的 *zhēnde*
reason 原因 *yuányīn*
receipt 收据 *shōujù*
recently 最近 *zuìjìn*
reception *(in hotel)* 前台 *qiántái*
» *(welcome party)* 招待会 *zhāodàihuì*
receptionist 服务员 *fúwùyuán*
recipe 菜谱 *càipǔ*
to **recognise** *(somebody)* 认出 *rènchū*
» *(Chinese characters)* 认识 *rènshí*
recommend 推荐 *tuījiàn*
red 红色 *hóngsè*
Red Cross 红十字会 *hóng shízìhuì*
to **reduce** 减少 *jiǎnshǎo*
red wine 红葡萄酒 *hóng pútáojiǔ*
to **refill** 加/添 *jiā/tiān*
refrigerator 冰箱 *bīngxiāng*
refugee 难民 *nànmín*
refund 退款 *tuìkuǎn*
region 地区 *dìqū*
to **register** 报名, 注册 *bàomíng, zhùcè*
relative 亲戚 *qīnqī*
relaxing 放松, 舒服 *fàngsōng, shūfú*
religion 宗教 *zōngjiào*
remains *(of old city)* 遗址 *yízhǐ*
to **remember** 记得 *jìde*
remote 偏僻 *piānpì*
to **remove** 除去 *chúqù*
to **rent** *(flat)* 房租 *fángzū*
» *(cars, bikes)* 租车费 *zū chē fèi*
to **repair** 修 *xiū*
to **repeat** 重复 *chóngfù*
to **reply** 回答 *huídá*
to **request** 请求 *qǐngqiú*
to **rescue** 救 *jiù*
reservation 预订 *yùdìng*
reserved 预订的 *yùdìngde*
restaurant 餐馆, 饭馆 *cānguǎn, fànguǎn*
rest-room 休息室 *xiūxí shì*
result 结果 *jiéguǒ*
retired 退休了 *tuìxiūle*
to **return** *(book)* 还 *huán*
» *(home)* 回 *huí*
return ticket 往返票 *wǎngfǎnpiào*
to **reverse** *(car)* 倒车 *dàochē*
reverse charge call 对方付款电话 *duìfāng fùkuǎn diànhuà*
rice 米饭 *mǐfàn*
rice wine 米酒 *mǐ jiǔ*
rich *(person)* 富, 有钱 *fù, yǒuqián*
» *(resources)* 丰富 *fēngfù*
to **ride** *(bycicle)* 骑 *qí*
ridiculous 荒唐, 可笑 *huāngtáng, kěxiào*
right *(not left)* 右 *yòu*
» *(correct)* 对 *duì*
right-handed 用右手做事 *yòng yòushǒu zuòshì*
ripe *(fruit)* 熟 *shóu*
rip-off 敲竹杠 *qiāo zhúgāng*
risk, risky 危险 *wéixiǎn*
river 河 *hé*
road 路 *lù*
roast 烤 *kǎo*
to **rob** 抢 *qiǎng*
robbery 抢劫 *qiǎngjié*
rock 石头 *shítóu*
romance 浪漫 *làngmàn*
roof 房顶 *fángdǐng*
room 房间 *fángjiān*
room service 房间服务 *fángjiān fúwù*
rope 绳子 *shéngzi*
rose 玫瑰 *méiguī*
rotten 烂了 *lànle*
rough *(surface)* 粗糙 *cūcào*
» *(behaviour)* 粗鲁 *cūlǔ*
round (adj) 圆 *yuán*

route 路线 *lùxiàn*
row *(theatre)* 排 *pái*
to row *(boat)* 划船 *huàchuán*
royal 皇家 *huángjiā*
rubber *(material)* 橡胶 *xiàngjiāo*
» *(eraser)* 橡皮 *xiàngpí*
rubbish *(waste)* 垃圾 *lājī*
rucksack 背包 *bèibāo*
rude 粗鲁, 没礼貌 *cūlǔ, méi lǐmào*
rug 小地毯 *xiǎo dìtǎn*
ruins 废墟 *fèixū*
ruler *(for measuring)* 尺子 *chǐzi*
to run 跑 *pǎo*
rush hour 上下班时间 *shàngxiàbān shíjiān*
Russia 俄国 *é'guó*
rusty 生锈的 *shēngxiùde*

S

sad 难过 *nánguò*
safe, safety 安全 *ānquán*
safe *(strongbox)* 保险柜 *bǎoxiǎn guì*
safety pin 别针 *bié zhēn*
to sail 航行 *hángxíng*
salad 色拉 *sèlā*
salary 工资 *gōngzī*
sale *(bargains)* 甩卖 *shuǎimài*
salesperson 推销员 *tuīxiāoyuán*
salmon 大马哈鱼 *dàmǎhāyú*
salt 盐 *yán*
salty 咸 *xián*
same 一样 *yīyàng*
sample 样本 *yàngběn*
sand 沙子 *shāzi*
sandals 凉鞋 *liángxié*
sandwich 三明治 *sānmíngzhì*
sanitary towel 卫生巾 *wèishēng jīn*
satisfactory 令人满意的 *lìngrén mǎnyìde*
sauce 汁, 酱 *zhī, jiàng*
saucepan 平底锅 *píngdǐguō*
saucer 碟子 *diézi*
sauna 蒸气浴 *zhēngqìyù*
sausage 香肠 *xiāngcháng*
to save *(life)* 救 *jiù*
to save *(money, time)* 节约 *jiéyuē*
to say 说 *shuō*
scales 秤 *chèng*
scarf 围巾 *wéijīn*
scenery 风景 *fēngjǐng*
schedule 日程 *rìchéng*
school 学校 *xuéxiào*
» primary school 小学 *xiǎo xué*
» secondary school 中学 *zhōng xué*
» university 大学 *dàxué*
science 科学 *kēxué*
scientist 科学家 *kēxuéjiā*
scissors 剪刀 *jiǎndāo*
scooter 独轮车 *dúlúnchē*
score 分数 *fēnshù*
Scotland 苏格兰 *sūgélán*
Scottish 苏格兰人 *sūgélánrén*
to scratch 抓一下, 刮一下 *zhuāyīxià, guāyīxià*
screen 屏幕 *píngmù*
screw 螺丝钉 *luósīdīng*
screwdriver 螺丝刀 *luósīdāo*
sculpture 雕塑 *diāosù*
sea 海 *hǎi*
seafood 海鲜 *hǎixiān*
seal *(name stamp)* 图章 *túzhāng*
to search 找 *zhǎo*
seasick 晕船 *yūnchuán*
season 季节 *jìjié*
season ticket 季度票 *jìdù piào*
seat 座位 *zuòwèi*
seat belt 安全带 *ānquán dài*
seaweed 海草 *hǎicǎo*
» *(edible)* 紫菜 *zǐcài*
second *(number)* 第二 *dì'èr*
» *(of time)* 秒 *miǎo*
second class 二等 *èr děng*

secret 秘密 *mìmì*
secretary 秘书 *mìshū*
to see 看见 *kànjiàn*
see you later 回见 *huí jiàn*
self-service 自助 *zì zhù*
to sell 卖 *mài*
senior 高级 *gāojí*
sense 感觉 *gǎnjué*
» it doesn't make sense 没道理 *méi dàolǐ*
sensible *(idea)* 有道理 *yǒudàolǐ*
» *(person)* 讲道理 *jiǎngdàolǐ*
sensitive 敏感 *mǐngǎn*
separate 分开 *fēnkāi*
serious 严重 *yánzhòng*
to serve 伺候 *cìhòu*
service *(sector)* 服务 *fúwù*
» *(charge)* 小费 *xiǎofèi*
service apartment 酒店公寓 *jiǔdiàn gōngyù*
serviette 餐巾 *cānjīn*
sesame 芝麻 *zhīmá*
» sesame oil 香油 *xiāng yóu*
set menu 套餐 *tào cān*
to set off 出发 *chūfā*
to sew 缝 *féng*
sex 性 *xìng*
sexy 性感 *xìnggǎn*
to shake hands 握手 *wò shǒu*
shallow *(water)* 浅 *qiǎn*
shame: what a shame! 真可惜 *zhēn kěxí*
shampoo 洗发液 *xǐfàyè*
to share 合用 *héyòng*
sharp *(knife)* 快 *kuài*
» *(pain)* 厉害 *lìhài*
to shave 刮 *guā*
shaving cream 剃须膏 *tìxū gāo*
she 她 *tā*
sheep 羊 *yáng*
sheet 纸 *zhǐ*
shelf 架子 *jiàzi*
shell 壳 *ké*
shiny 发亮 *fāliàng*
ship 船 *chuán*
shirt 衬衣 *chènyī*
shock 吃惊 *chījīng*
shoe 鞋子 *xiézi*
» shoelace 鞋带 *xiédài*
» shoe polish 鞋油 *xié yóu*
» shoe repairer 修鞋店 *xiūxié diàn*
shop 商店 *shāngdiàn*
shopping 买东西 *mǎidōngxī*
shopping centre 商业中心 *shāngyè zhōngxīn*
shorts 短裤 *duǎnkù*
shoulder 肩膀 *jiānbǎng*
to shout 喊 *hǎn*
to show 演示 *yǎnshì*
shower *(wash)* 淋浴 *línyù*
» *(rain)* 阵雨 *zhènyǔ*
showercap 淋浴帽 *línyùmào*
to shut 关 *guān*
shut up! 住嘴 *zhùzuǐ*
shy 害羞 *hàixiū*
Sichuan food 川菜 *chuān cài*
sick 生病, 呕吐 *shēngbìng, ǒutǔ*
side 边 *biān*
sightseeing 观光 *guānguāng*
sign 标志 *biāozhì*
to sign, signature 签名/签字 *qiānmíng/ qiānzì*
signal 信号 *xìnhào*
signpost 路标 *lùbiāo*
silence, silent 沉默 *chénmò*
silk 丝绸 *sīchóu*
silly 笨, 蠢 *bèn, chǔn*
silver 银 *yín*
SIM card SIM 卡 *SIM kǎ*
similar 相同 *xiāngtóng*
simple 简单 *jiǎndān*
sin 罪过 *zuìguò*

to sing 唱歌 *chànggē*
Singapore 新加坡 *xīnjiāpō*
single *(room)* 单人 *dānrén*
» *(person)* 单身 *dānshēn*
» *(ticket)* 单程 *dānchéng*
sink 水池 *shuǐchí*
sir 先生 *xiānshēng*
sister *(elder)* 姐姐 *jiějie*
» *(younger)* 妹妹 *mèimei*
to sit 坐 *zuò*
size 号码，尺寸 *hàomǎ, chǐcùn*
to ski, skiing 滑雪 *huáxuě*
skimmed milk 脱脂奶 *tuōzhī nǎi*
skin 皮肤 *pífū*
skirt 裙子 *qúnzi*
sky 天 *tiān*
to sleep 睡觉 *shuìjiào*
sleeper, sleeping-car 卧铺车厢 *wòpù chēxiāng*
sleeping pill 安眠药 *ānmián yào*
sleepy 困 *kùn*
sleeve 袖子 *xiùzi*
slice 片 *piàn*
slim 苗条 *miáotiáo*
slippery 滑 *huá*
slow, slowly 慢 *màn*
small 小 *xiǎo*
smell 味儿 *wèir*
smile 微笑 *wéixiào*
smoke 吸烟/抽烟 *xīyān/chōuyān*
smooth 顺利 *shùnlì*
snack bar 快餐店 *kuàicān diàn*
snake 蛇 *shé*
to sneeze 打喷嚏 *dǎ pēntì*
snob 势利眼 *shìliyǎn*
snorkel 潜水吸气管 *qiánshuǐ xīqì guǎn*
snow 雪 *xuě*
to snow 下雪 *xiàxuě*
so *(therefore)* 所以 *suǒyǐ*
» *(extremely)* 这么 *zhème*
soap 香皂/肥皂 *xiāngzào/féizào*
socialism 社会主义 *shèhuìzhǔyì*
society 社会 *shèhuì*
socks 袜子 *wàzi*
soda 苏打 *sūdǎ*
soft 软 *ruǎn*
soft drinks 软饮料 *ruǎn yǐnliào*
software 软件 *ruǎnjiàn*
soldier 士兵 *shìbīng*
solicitor 律师 *lǜshī*
solid *(not liquid)* 固体 *gùtǐ*
» *(strong)* 结实 *jiéshí*
some 一些 *yīxiē*
somebody, someone 有人 *yǒurén*
somehow 不知怎么 *bùzhīzěnme*
something 有件事，有些事 *yǒujiànshì, yǒuxiēshì*
sometimes 有时候 *yǒushíhòu*
somewhere 某地 *mǒudì*
son 儿子 *érzi*
song 歌 *gē*
soon 马上 *mǎshàng*
sorry 对不起 *duìbùqǐ*
sound 声音 *shēngyīn*
soup 汤 *tāng*
sour 酸 *suān*
south 南 *nán*
souvenir 纪念品 *jìniànpǐn*
space 空间 *kōngjiān*
spare 多余的 *duōyúde*
sparkling 带汽的 *dàiqìde*
to speak 说，讲 *shuō, jiǎng*
special 特别 *tèbié*
speciality 专业 *zhuānyè*
spectacles 眼镜 *yǎnjìng*
speed 速度 *sùdù*
speed limit 速度限制 *sùdù xiànzhì*
to spell *(a word)* 拼 *pīn*
to spend *(money)* 花 *huā*
» *(time)* 过 *guò*
spice 调料 *tiáoliào*

spicy 辣 *là*
spider 蜘蛛 *zhīzhū*
spirit *(drink)* 烈酒 *lièjiǔ*
splinter 刺, 尖片 *cì, jiānpiàn*
to spoil 毁了 *huǐle*
sponge 海绵 *hǎimián*
spoon 勺子 *sháozi*
sport 运动 *yùndòng*
spot *(on face)* 粉刺 *fěncì*
spouse 爱人/配偶 *àirén/pèi'ǒu*
sprained 扭伤了 *niǔshāngle*
to spray 洒/喷 *sǎ/pēn*
spring onion 洋葱 *yáng cōng*
square *(open space)* 广场 *guǎngchǎng*
» *(shape)* 方 *fāng*
stadium 室内体育馆 *shìnèi tǐyùguǎn*
stain 污点 *wūdiǎn*
stairs 楼梯 *lóutī*
stall 摊/亭 *tān/tíng*
stamps 邮票 *yóupiào*
to stand 站着 *zhànzhe*
standard 标准 *biāozhǔn*
star *(in the sky)* 星星 *xīngxīng*
» *(celebrity)* 明星 *míngxīng*
to stare 盯着 *dīngzhe*
to start 开始 *kāishǐ*
starter *(meal)* 头盘 *tóupán*
starving 饿死了 *èsǐle*
state *(in USA)* 州 *zhōu*
station 车站 *chēzhàn*
stationer's 文具店 *wénjù diàn*
statue 塑像 *sùxiàng*
to stay 待/呆 *dāi*
steak 牛排 *niúpái*
to steal 偷 *tōu*
steamed 蒸的 *zhēngde*
steel 钢 *gāng*
steep 陡 *dǒu*
stereo 立体声 *lìtǐshēng*
sticky 黏 *nián*
stiff 硬梆梆 *yìng bāngbāng*
still 仍然 *réngrán*
to sting 螫 *zhē*
to stir-fry 炒 *chǎo*
stock exchange 股票市场 *gǔpiào shìchǎng*
stolen 偷来的 *tōuláide*
stomach-ache 胃疼/肚子疼 *wèi téng/dùzi téng*
stone 石头 *shítóu*
to stop 停 *tíng*
storm 暴风雨 *bàofēngyǔ*
storey 楼层 *lóucéng*
story 故事 *gùshì*
straight 直 *zhí*
» **straight on** 直走 *zhí zǒu*
» **straight ahead** 一直往前 *yīzhí wǎngqián*
strange 奇怪 *qíguài*
stranger 生人 *shēngrén*
strap 带, 皮带 *dài, pídài*
straw *(drinking)* 吸管 *xīguǎn*
street 街 *jiē*
stripe 条纹 *tiáowén*
strong *(person or thing)* 壮/结实 *zhuàng/jiéshí*
» *(taste)* 浓 *nóng*
stuck 卡住了 *kǎzhùle*
student 学生 *xuéshēng*
to study 学习 *xuéxí*
stupid 笨 *bèn*
style *(clothing)* 式样 *shìyàng*
subtitles 字幕 *zìmù*
suburb 郊区 *jiāoqū*
suddenly 突然 *túrán*
sugar 糖 *táng*
suggestion 建议 *jiànyì*
suit 套装 *tàozhuāng*
to suit: it suits you 这适合你 *zhè shìhé nǐ*
suitable 合适 *héshì*

suitcase 手提箱 *shǒutíxiāng*
sun 太阳 *tàiyáng*
to sunbathe 晒太阳 *shàitàiyáng*
sunburn 晒伤的皮肤 *shàishāng de pífū*
sunglasses 太阳眼镜 *tàiyáng yǎnjìng*
sunrise 日出 *rìchū*
sunstroke 中暑 *zhòngshǔ*
suntan 晒后发黑的肤色 *shàihòu fāhēi de fūsè*
suntan lotion 防晒油 *fángshài yóu*
super 超 *chāo*
superb 好极了 *hǎojíle*
supermarket 超级市场 *chāojí shìchǎng*
supper 晚饭 *wǎnfàn*
supplement 补充 *bǔchōng*
suppose: I suppose so 我想是这样 *wǒxiǎng shì zhèyàng*
suppository 拴剂 *shuānjì*
sure 确信 *quèxìn*
surface 表面 *biǎomiàn*
surname 姓 *xìng*
surprise 惊讶 *jīngyà*
to swallow 咽/吞 *yàn/tūn*
to sweat 出汗 *chūhàn*
sweater 毛衣 *máoyī*
to sweep 清扫 *qīsǎo*
sweet 甜 *tián*
sweet and sour 糖醋 *táng cù*
sweetener 增甜剂 *zēngtiánjì*
sweets 水果糖 *shuǐguǒtáng*
to swell 肿 *zhǒng*
to swim, swimming 游泳 *yóuyǒng*
swimming pool 游泳池 *yóuyǒng chí*
swimming trunks, swimsuit 游泳衣 *yóuyǒng yī*
to switch on 开 *kāi*
to switch off 关 *guān*
swollen 肿了 *zhǒngle*
sympathy 同情 *tóngqíng*
symptom 症状 *zhèngzhuàng*
synagogue 犹太教堂 *yóutài jiàotáng*
synthetic 人造的 *rénzàode*
system 体系，制度 *tǐxì, zhìdù*

T

table 桌子 *zhuōzi*
table tennis 乒乓球 *pīngpāng qiú*
tailor 裁缝 *cáiféng*
to take 拿 *ná*
to take off 起飞 *qǐ fēi*
to take a photograph 照相/拍照 *zhào xiàng/pāi zhào*
to talk 说话 *shuōhuà*
tall 高 *gāo*
tampons 月经棉塞 *yuèjīng miánsāi*
Taoism 道教 *dàojiào*
tap 水龙头 *shuǐlóngtóu*
tank 坦克 *tǎnkè*
tangerine 桔子 *júzi*
tape measure 皮尺子 *pí chǐzi*
to taste 尝 *cháng*
tax 税收 *shuìshōu*
taxi 出租车 *chūzūchē*
taxi rank 出租车站 *chūzūchē zhàn*
tea 茶 *chá*
» **tea house** 茶馆 *chá guǎn*
teabag 茶袋 *chádài*
to teach 教 *jiāo*
teacher 老师/教师 *lǎoshī/jiàoshī*
teacup 茶杯 *chábēi*
team 小组 *xiǎozǔ*
teapot 茶壶 *cháhú*
to tear *(rip)* 撕开 *sīkāi*
teaspoon 茶勺 *chásháo*
technology 科技 *kējì*
teenager 青少年 *qīngshàonián*
telephone 电话 *diànhuà*
to telephone 打电话 *dǎ diànhuà*
» **telephone card** 电话卡 *diànhuà kǎ*
television 电视 *diànshì*

to tell 告诉 *gàosù*
temperature 气温 *qìwēn*
» *(fever)* 发烧 *fāshāo*
temple 庙 *miào*
temporary 临时 *línshí*
tennis 网球 *wǎngqiú*
tennis court 网球场 *wǎngqiú chǎng*
tent 帐篷 *zhàngpéng*
terminal *(airport)* 航站楼 *hángzhànlóu*
terrace 台阶, 看台 *táijiē, kàntái*
terrible 糟透了 *zāotòule*
terrific 棒极了 *bàngjíle*
terrorist 恐怖份子 *kǒngbùfènzi*
text message 短信 *duǎn xìn*
Thailand 泰国 *tàiguó*
thanks, thank you 谢谢 *xièxie*
that 那, 那个 *nà, nàge*
theatre 剧院 *jùyuàn*
their, theirs 他们的 *tāmende*
them 他们 *tāmen*
then 然后 *ránhòu*
there 那儿 *nàr*
therefore 因此 *yīncǐ*
thermometer 温度计, 体温表 *wēndùjì, tǐwēnbiǎo*
these 这些 *zhèxiē*
they 他们 *tāmen*
thick 厚 *hòu*
thief 小偷 *xiǎotōu*
thigh 大腿 *dàtuǐ*
thin 瘦 *shòu*
thing 东西 *dōngxi*
to think 想 *xiǎng*
thirsty 渴 *kě*
this morning 今天早上 *jīntiān zǎoshàng*
this week 这个星期 *zhège xīngqī*
this year 今年 *jīn nián*
those 那些 *nàxiē*
thousand 千 *qiān*
throat lozenges 清喉药 *qīnghóu yào*
through 经过 *jīngguò*
to throw away 扔掉 *rěng diào*
thunder 雷 *léi*
Tibet 西藏 *xīzàng*
ticket 票 *piào*
ticket office 售票处 *shòupiào chǔ*
tidy 整洁 *zhěngjié*
tie 领带 *lǐngdài*
tight 紧 *jǐn*
tights 连裤袜 *liánkùwà*
time 时间 *shíjiān*
» what time is it? 几点了 *jǐ diǎn le*
timetable 时刻表 *shíkèbiǎo*
tin 罐头 *guàntóu*
tin-opener 罐头起子 *guàntóu qǐzi*
tiny *(size)* 很小 *hěnxiǎo*
» *(quantity)* 很少 *hěnshǎo*
tip 小费 *xiǎofèi*
tired 累 *lèi*
tissues 面巾纸 *miànjīnzhǐ*
to have a toast 祝酒 *zhùjiǔ*
tobacco 烟草 *yāncǎo*
tobacconist's 烟草店 *yāncǎo diàn*
today 今天 *jīntiān*
tofu 豆腐 *dòufǔ*
together 一起 *yīqǐ*
toilet paper 卫生纸 *wèishēng zhǐ*
toiletries 卫生用品 *wèishēng yòngpǐn*
toilets 厕所 *cèsuǒ*
toll 使用费 *shǐyòngfèi*
tomato 西红柿 *xīhóngshì*
tomorrow 明天 *míngtiān*
tongue 舌头 *shétóu*
tonight 今天晚上 *jīntiān wǎnshàng*
tonsils 扁桃腺 *biǎntáoxiàn*
too *(extremely)* 太 *tài*
» *(also)* 也 *yě*
tool 工具 *gōngjù*
tooth 牙 *yá*
» toothache 牙疼 *yáténg*

» **toothbrush** 牙刷 *yáshuā*
» **toothpaste** 牙膏 *yágāo*
» **toothpick** 牙签 *yáqiān*
top *(on top of)* 在.....上头 *zài..... shàng tóu*
torch 电筒 *diàntǒng*
torn 撕破了 *sīpòle*
total 总数 *zǒngshù*
totally 完全 *wánquán*
to touch 触摸 *chùmō*
to be touched *(moved)* 感动 *gǎndòng*
tough *(meat)* 老 *lǎo*
» *(difficult)* 不容易 *bùróngyì*
to tour 观光 *guānguāng*
tourist 游客 *yóukè*
tourist guide 导游 *dǎoyóu*
towards 朝 *cháo*
towel 毛巾 *máojīn*
tower 塔 *tǎ*
town 城 *chéng*
» **town centre** 市中心 *shì zhōngxīn*
» **town hall** 市政厅 *shìzhèng tīng*
toy 玩具 *wánjù*
tradition, traditional 传统 *chuántǒng*
traffic 交通 *jiāotōng*
» **traffic jam** 交通堵塞 *jiāotōng dǔsè*
» **traffic light** 红绿灯 *hónglǜ dēng*
tram 电车 *diànchē*
train 火车 *huǒchē*
» **by train** 坐火车 *zuò huǒchē*
trainers 运动鞋 *yùndòngxié*
tranquilliser 镇静药 *zhènjìngyào*
to translate, translator 翻译 *fānyì*
translation 翻译 *fānyì*
to travel 旅游 *lǚyóu*
travel agent 旅行社 *lǚxíng shè*
traveller's cheque 旅行支票 *lǚxíng zhīpiào*
travel sickness 晕车, 晕船, 晕机 *yūn chē, yūn chuán, yūn jī*
treatment *(medical)* 治疗 *zhìliáo*
tree 树 *shù*
trendy 时髦 *shímáo*
tricky 难办 *nánbàn*
trip 旅行, 一路 *lǚxíng, yīlù*
tropical 热带 *rèdài*
trouble 麻烦 *máfán*
trousers 裤子 *kùzi*
true 真的 *zhēnde*
truth 实话, 事实 *shíhuà, shìshí*
to try 试图 *shìtú*
to try on 试试 *shìshi*
T-shirt 体恤衫 *tǐxù shān*
tunnel 隧道 *suìdào*
turkey 火鸡 *huǒjī*
to turn 拐弯 *guǎiwān*
to turn off 关掉 *guān diào*
turn: it's my turn 轮到我了 *lúndào wǒ le*
TV 电视 *diànshì*
twice 两次 *liǎngcì*
twin beds 两个单人床 *liǎng ge dāngrén chuáng*
twins 双胞胎 *shuāngbāotāi*
twisted 扭成一团 *niǔchéng yītuán*
to type 打字 *dǎzì*
typical 典型 *diǎnxíng*
tyre 轮胎 *lúntāi*

U

ugly 难看 *nánkàn*
ulcer 溃疡 *kuìyáng*
umbrella 雨伞 *yǔsǎn*
uncomfortable 不舒服 *bùshūfú*
under 在....底下 *zài....dǐxià*
underdone *(meal)* 不熟 *bùshóu*
underground *(rail)* 地铁 *dìtiě*
underpants 内裤 *nèikù*
to understand 懂 *dǒng*
understanding 理解 *lǐjiě*
underwear 内衣 *nèiyī*

to undress 脱衣服 *tuō yīfú*
unemployed 失业 *shīyè*
unfair 不公平 *bùgōngpíng*
unfortunately 不幸的 *búxìngde*
unhappy 不高兴 *bùgāoxìng*
uniform 制服 *zhìfú*
United States 美国 *měi guó*
university 大学 *dàxué*
unleaded petrol 不含铅的汽油 *bù hánqiān de qìyóu*
unless 除非 *chúfēi*
to unlock 打开 *dǎkāi*
unpleasant 不愉快 *bù yúkuài*
to unscrew 拧开 *níngkāi*
unwell 不舒服 *bù shūfú*
until 直到 *zhídào*
unusual 不常见 *bù chángjiàn*
up 上 *shàng*
upmarket 高档 *gāodǎng*
upper 上面 *shàngmiàn*
upset 不安 *bùān*
upset stomach 胃不舒服 *wèi bùshūfú*
upstairs 楼上 *lóushàng*
urgent 急 *jí*
urine 尿 *niào*
us 我们 *wǒmen*
USB lead U盘联线 *U pán liánxiàn*
to use 用 *yòng*
used 用过的 *yòngguòde*
useful 有用 *yǒuyòng*
useless 没用处 *méiyòngchù*
usual, usually 平常 *píngcháng*

V

vacancy *(at hotel)* 空房间 *kòng fángjiān*
» *(job)* 空缺 *kòngquē*
vacation 假期 *jiàqī*
vagina 阴道 *yīndào*
valid *(ticket)* 有效 *yǒuxiào*
valley 山谷 *shāngǔ*
valuables 贵重的 *guìzhòngde*
value 价值 *jiàzhí*
van 运货车 *yùnhuòchē*
variety 多种 *duōzhǒng*
vary 不一样 *bùyīyàng*
vase 花瓶 *huāpíng*
VAT 增值税 *zēng zhí shuì*
vegan 严格素食者 *yángé sùshízhě*
vegetables 蔬菜 *shūcài*
vegetarian 吃素 *chīsù*
vegetarian food 素菜/素食 *sù cài/sù shí*
vehicle 车辆 *chēliàng*
very 很 *hěn*
very much 十分 *shífēn*
vet 兽医 *shòuyī*
view 景色 *jǐngsè*
village 村子 *cūnzi*
vinegar 醋 *cù*
virgin 处女 *chǔnǚ*
visa 签证 *qiānzhèng*
visibility 能见度 *néngjiàndù*
to visit 参观 *cānguān*
visitor 参观者 *cānguānzhě*
vitamin 维生素 *wéishēngsù*
voice 声音 *shēngyīn*
volleyball 排球 *páiqiú*
voltage 电压 *diànyā*
to vomit 吐 *tù*

W

wage 工资 *gōngzī*
to wait 等 *děng*
waiter, waitress 服务员/招待员 *fúwùyuán/zhāodàiyuán*
waiting room *(train station)* 候车室 *hòuchē shì*
» *(hospital)* 候诊室 *hòuzhēn shì*
to wake up 叫醒, 醒来 *jiào xǐng, xǐnglái*
Wales 威尔士 *wēi'ěrshì*

walk 走路 *zǒulù*
wall (inside) 墙 *qiáng*
wallet 钱包 *qiánbāo*
to want 想 *xiǎng*
war 战争 *zhànzhēng*
warm *(weather)* 暖和 *nuǎnhé*
» *(person)* 好心 *hǎoxīn*
warning 警告 *jǐnggào*
to wash, washing 洗 *xǐ*
wash basin 洗手池 *xǐshǒu chí*
washing machine 洗衣机 *xǐyī jī*
washing powder 洗衣粉 *xǐyī fěn*
washing-up 洗碗 *xǐwǎn*
washing-up liquid 洗碗液 *xǐwǎn yè*
wasp 黄蜂 *huángfēng*
to waste 浪费 *làngfèi*
wastepaper basket 垃圾框 *lājī kuāng*
watch 手表 *shǒubiǎo*
to watch 看/观看 *kàn/guānkàn*
water 水 *shuǐ*
watercolour 水彩画 *shuǐcǎihuà*
waterfall 瀑布 *pùbù*
waterproof 防水 *fángshuǐ*
wave *(sea)* 海浪 *hǎilàng*
wax 蜡 *là*
way *(route)* 路 *lù*
» *(method)* 办法 *bànfǎ*
way out 出口 *chūkǒu*
we 我们 *wǒmen*
weak *(drink)* 淡 *dàn*
» *(person)* 弱 *ruò*
wealthy 富 *fù*
to wear 穿 *chuān*
weather 天气 *tiānqì*
weather forecast 天气预报 *tiānqì yùbào*
web *(Internet)* 网络 *wǎngluò*
web designer 网络设计者 *wǎngluò shèjìzhě*
wedding 婚礼 *hūnlǐ*
week 星期 *xīngqī*
weekday 周一至周五 *zhōuyī zhì zhōuwǔ*
weekend 周末 *zhōumò*
weekly 每周一次的 *měizhōu yīcìde*
weight 重量 *zhòngliàng*
welcome: you're welcome 不客气 *bú kèqì*
to welcome 欢迎 *huānyíng*
well-done *(meat)* 老一点 *lǎo yīdiǎn*
well done *(good work)* 做得不错 *zuò de búcuò*
Welsh 威尔士 *wēi'ěrshì*
west 西 *xī*
western 西方的 *xīfāngde*
western food 西餐 *xī cān*
western-style 西式 *xī shì*
wet 湿 *shī*
what 什么 *shénme*
what date...? 几号 *jǐ hào*
what day...? 星期几 *xīngqī jǐ*
what time...? 几点 *jǐ diǎn*
wheel 轮子 *lúnzi*
wheelchair 轮椅 *lúnyǐ*
when 什么时候 *shénme shíhòu*
where 哪儿 *nǎr*
whereabouts 哪里 *nǎlǐ*
which 哪个 *nǎge*
while: for a while 一会儿 *yīhuìr*
whisky 威士忌 *wēishìjì*
to whisper 小声说/悄悄说 *xiǎoshēng shuō/qiāoqiao shuō*
white 白 *bái*
white wine 白葡萄酒 *bái pútáojiǔ*
who 谁 *shéi*
whole 整个 *zhěnggè*
whose 谁的 *shéide*
why 为什么 *wéishénme*
wide 宽 *kuān*
widow 寡妇 *guǎfù*
widower 鳏夫 *guānfū*

wife 妻子/太太/夫人 *qīzi/tàitai/fūrén*
wig 假发 *jiǎfà*
to win 赢 *yíng*
wind 风 *fēng*
window 窗户 *chuānghù*
to windsurf 做帆板运动 *zuò fānbǎn yùndòng*
windy 刮风了 *guāfēngle*
wine 葡萄酒 *pútáojiǔ*
wine glass 葡萄酒杯 *pútáojiǔ bēi*
to wish 希望 *xīwàng*
with 和, 跟 *hé, gēn*
without 没有 *méiyǒu*
witness 证人 *zhèngrén*
witty 诙谐 *huīxié*
woman, women 女的/女人 *nǚde/nǚrén*
women's toilet 女厕所 *nǚ cèsuǒ*
wonderful 好极了 *hǎojíle*
wonton soup 馄饨汤 *húntún tāng*
wood 木头 *mùtóu*
woods 树林 *shùlín*
wool 羊毛 *yángmáo*
word 词 *cí*
work, to work 工作 *gōngzuò*
» it doesn't work 坏了 *huài le*
working-class 工人阶级 *gōngrén jiējí*
world 世界 *shìjiè*
worried 着急 *zháojí*
worry: don't worry 别急 *bié jí*
worse 差 *chā*
wounded (injured) 受伤了 *shòushāngle*
to wrap up 包起来 *bāo qǐlái*
to write 写 *xiě*
writer 作家 *zuòjiā*
wrong 错 *cuò*
» what's wrong? 怎么了 *zěnme le*

X

X-ray X-光 *X-guāng*

Y

Yangtze River 长江 *cháng jiāng*
year 年 *nián*
yellow 黄 *huáng*
Yellow River 黄河 *huáng hé*
yes 是的 *shìde*
yesterday 昨天 *zuótiān*
yet: not yet 还没有 *hái méiyǒu*
yoghurt 酸奶 *suānnǎi*
you (singular) 你 *nǐ*
» (plural) 你们 *nǐmen*
young 年轻 *niánqīng*
your, yours (singular) 你的 *nǐde*
» (plural) 你们的 *nǐmende*
youth 青春 *qīngchūn*
youth hostel 青年旅社 *qīngnián lǚshè*
yuan *(Chinese currency)* 元 *yuán*

Z

zero 零 *líng*
zip 拉链 *lāliàn*
zoo 动物园 *dòngwùyuán*
zoom lens 可变焦距镜头 *kěbiàn jiāojù jìngtóu*

Chinese – English Dictionary

A

ài 爱 to love

ài'ěrlán 爱尔兰 Ireland

ài'ěrlánrén 爱尔兰人 Irish *(people)*

àihào 爱好 hobby

àirén 爱人 spouse

àishàngle 爱上了 to fall in love

áizhèng 癌症 cancer

àizī bìngdú yángxìng 艾滋病毒阳性 HIV positive

àizībìng 艾滋病 AIDS

ānquán 安全 safe, safety

ānquán dài 安全带 seat belt

ānquán jiǎnchá 安全检查 security check

āsīpǐlín 阿斯匹林 aspirin

B

bà 把 handle

bàba 爸爸 dad, daddy

bàgōng 罢工 strike

bái 白 white

bǎi 百 hundred

bái mǐfàn 白米饭 boiled rice

bái pútáojiǔ 白葡萄酒 white wine

bànge 半个 half (n)

bāngzhù 帮助 to help

bànlǐ dēngjī shǒuxù 办理登机手续 to check in *(at airport)*

bànlǐ líkāi shǒuxù 办理离开手续 to check out *(at hotel)*

bāo 包 bag

bǎobèir 宝贝儿 darling, sweetheart

bǎoxiǎn 保险 insurance

bǎoxiǎnguì 保险柜 safe *(strongbox)*

bàoyuàn 抱怨 to complain

bāozā 包扎 bandage

bèi dǎbǔ 被逮捕 under arrest

bèibāo 背包 rucksack

biǎogé 表格 form *(document)*

biāozhì 标志 sign

bīng jī lín 冰激淋 ice cream

bǐnggān 饼干 biscuit

bìngle 病了 ill

bīnguǎn 宾馆 guest house, hotel

bìyùntào 避孕套 condom

bōlíbēi 玻璃杯 glass *(for drinks)*

bú kèqì 不客气 welcome: you're welcome

bù shūfú 不舒服 unwell

bù yǔnxǔde 不允许的 forbidden

bùgōngpíng 不公平 unfair

bùliào 布料 fabric

bùmén 部门 department *(corporate)*

bùróngyì 不容易 not easy, tough

bùshóu 不熟 underdone *(meal)*

bùshūfú 不舒服 uncomfortable

bùtóngyì 不同意 to disagree

bùxiāohuà 不消化 indigestion

bùxǐhuān 不喜欢 to dislike

búzhèngshì 不正式 informal

C

cài 菜 dish *(food)*

cáiféng 裁缝 tailor

cānguǎn 餐馆 restaurant

cānguān 参观 to visit

cāngyíng 苍蝇 fly *(insect)*

cánjí 残疾 disabled
cānjù 餐具 cutlery
cǎoyào 草药 herb
cèsuǒ 厕所 toilets, lavatory
chá 茶 tea
cháng 尝 to taste
cháng chéng 长城 Great Wall
cháng jiāng 长江 Yangtze River
chángtú 长途 long distance
chángtúchē 长途车 coach
chǎo 炒 to stir-fry
cháodài 朝代 dynasty
chāojí shìchǎng 超级市场 supermarket
cháoxiān 朝鲜 Korea
cháshāo 茶勺 teaspoon
chāzi 叉子 fork
chē 车 car
chéng 城 town
chéngrén 成人 adult
chéngshì 城市 city
chéngwéi 成为 to become
chēxiāng 车厢 carriage *(train)*
chēzhàn 车站 station
chī 吃 to eat
chǐcùn 尺寸 size
chīsù 吃素 vegetarian
chōng xǐ 冲洗 to develop *(film)*
chōngdiànqì 充电器 charger *(phone)*
chōuyān 抽烟 to smoke, smoking
chuán sòng dài 传送带 conveyor belt
chuáng 床 bed
chuáng dān 床单 bed sheet, linen
chuānghù 窗户 window
chuānglián 窗帘 curtain
chuántǒng 传统 tradition, traditional
chuánzhēn 传真 fax
chūchāi 出差 to be on a business trip
chūhàn 出汗 to sweat
chuī 吹 to blow
chuī fēngjī 吹风机 hair dryer
chūkǒu 出口 exit, export, to export
chūxué zhě 初学者 beginner
chūzūchē 出租车 taxi
cí 词 word
cídiǎn 词典 dictionary
cìpǐn 次品 faulty
cūlǔ 粗鲁 rude, rough *(behaviour)*
cúnyīshì 存衣室 cloakroom
cūnzi 村子 village
cuòwù 错误 error, mistake

D

dà 大 large, big
dǎ bàn 打扮 to dress up
dǎ diànhuà 打电话 to telephone
dáfù 答复 answer
dàhuì 大会 conference
dǎhuǒjī 打火机 lighter *(cigarette)*
dàifū 大夫 doctor
dàlóu 大楼 building
dàmén 大门 gate, entrance
dāngxīn 当心 careful, caution
dāo 刀 knife
dàojiào 道教 Taoism
dàshǐguǎn 大使馆 embassy
dàxué 大学 university
dǎzhé 打折 discount
diànhuà 电话 telephone
diànhuà kǎ 电话卡 telephone card
diànhuà qūhào 电话区号 dialling code
diànnǎo 电脑 computer
diànshì 电视 TV

diàntī 电梯 escalator, lift
diàntǒng 电筒 torch
diànyǐngyuàn 电影院 cinema
diànzi yóujiàn 电子邮件 email
dìngpiào chù 订票处 booking office
dìzhèn 地震 earthquake
dǒng 懂 to understand
dōng 东 east
dōngfāngde 东方的 eastern
dǒngshì huì 董事会 board of directors
dòngwù 动物 animal
dòngwùyuán 动物园 zoo
duǎn xìn 短信 text message
dǔbó 赌博 gambling
duì 对 correct
duì huàn lǜ 兑换率 exchange rate
duì huánjìng yǒuyìde 对环境有益的 environmentally friendly
duì...guòmǐn 对... 过敏 allergic to
duìbùqǐ 对不起 excuse me, sorry
duìhuà 对话 dialogue, conversation
dùjià 度假 holiday
duō dà le 多大了 how old?
duō jiǔ 多久 how long?
duō shǎo 多少 how many?
duō yuǎn 多远 how far?
duōlù chāzuò 多路插座 adaptor
duōméitǐ guāngpán 多媒体光盘 CD-Rom
duōshǎo qián 多少钱 how much?
DVD jī DVD机 DVD player

E

è 饿 to be hungry
é'guó 俄国 Russia
ěrjī 耳机 headphones
értóng 儿童 children

F

fā diànzi yóujiàn 发电子邮件 to email
fāchē 发车 to depart *(train/bus)*
fákuǎn 罚款 fine *(penalty)*
fǎlǜ 法律 law
fàn 饭 food
fàndiàn 饭店 hotel
fànguǎn 饭馆 restaurant
fāngxiàng 方向 direction
fángzi 房子 house
fānù 发怒 angry
fānyì 翻译 to translate, translation
fāyán 发炎 infection
fēijīchǎng 飞机场 airport
fèiwù 废物 litter *(rubbish)*
fèiyòng 费用 expense
fēngjǐng 风景 scenery
féngzhì 缝制 sewing
fénmù 坟墓 grave *(cemetery)*
fēnshù 分数 score
fěnsī 粉丝 fan *(supporter)*
fó 佛 Buddha
fójiào 佛教 Buddhism
fójiào sìyuàn 佛教寺院 Buddhist temple
fójiàotú 佛教徒 Buddhist
fù 富 wealthy
fūqī 夫妻 married couple
fùyǒu 富有 rich
fùzá 复杂 complicated
fúzhuāng 服装 clothing

G

gài 盖 to build
gān bēi 干杯 Cheers!

gǎngbì 港币 Hong Kong dollar
gānjìng 干净 clean
gāo'ěrfū 高儿夫 golf
gāo'ěrfū qiúchǎng 高尔夫球场 golf course
gāojí 高级 senior, advanced
gāoxìng 高兴 happy
gē 歌 song
gèngyī shì 更衣室 changing room
gòngchǎn zhǔyì 共产主义 communism
gōngchǎng 工厂 factory
gōnggòng qìchē 公共汽车 bus
gōnggòng qìchē zhàn 公共汽车站 bus stop
gōngsī 公司 firm, company
gōngsī zǒngcái 公司总裁 CEO
gōngxǐ 恭喜 Congratulations!
gōngzī 工资 wage, salary
gōngzuò 工作 to work, job
guǎngdōnghuà 广东话 Cantonese
guāngpán 光盘 CD
guānguāng 观光 to tour, sightseeing
guì 贵 expensive
guǐ 鬼 ghost
guìzhòngde 贵重的 valuables
gùkè 顾客 customer
guójì 国际 international
guójiā 国家 country
guónèi 国内 domestic
guówài 国外 abroad
gǔpiào shìchǎng 股票市场 stock exchange
gùyuán 雇员 employee
gùzhǔ 雇主 employer

H

hǎi 海 sea
hǎicǎo 海草 seaweed
hǎixiān 海鲜 seafood
hángkōng gōngsī 航空公司 airline
hángkōng xìn 航空信 air mail
hánguó 韩国 South Korea
hànyǔ 汉语 Chinese *(language)*
hǎochī, 好吃 delicious
hǎohào wánr 好好玩儿 fun: to have fun
háohuá 豪华 luxury
hǎojíle 好极了 wonderful, superb
hàokè 好客 hospitality
hé 河 river
hē 喝 to drink
hé fàn 盒饭 box lunch
héfǎ 合法 legal
hēisè 黑色 black
hèn 恨 hate
hěn 很 very
hěnshǎo 很少 tiny *(quantity)*
hěnxiǎo 很小 *(size)*
hésè 褐色 brown
hétóng 合同 contract
hóngsè 红色 red
hóngshuǐ 洪水 flood
huángdì 皇帝 emperor
huángjiā 皇家 royal
huánjìng 环境 environment
huānyíng 欢迎 to welcome
huāyuán 花园 garden
huí jiàn 回见 see you later
huìyì 会议 meeting, conference
hùliánwǎng 互联网 internet
hūnlǐ 婚礼 wedding
huòbì 货币 currency

huǒchē 火车 train
huǒchē piào 火车票 train ticket

I

IP sì IP四 iPod

J

jí 急 urgent
jǐ 挤 crowded
jǐ 几 how many? *(small number)*
jǐ diǎn 几点 what time...?
jǐ diǎn le 几点了 what time is it?
jǐ hào 几号 what date...?
jiànkāng 健康 healthy, fit
jiāojuǎn 胶卷 film *(for camera)*
jiāoyóu 郊游 excursion
jiàoyù 教育 education
jiérì 节日 festival
jièshào 介绍 to introduce
jìjié 季节 season
jìn 近 to be closed
jīngjù 京剧 Beijing (Peking) Opera
jìngpiàn 镜片 lens, contact lenses
jǐngsè 景色 view
jīngshāng 经商 to do business
jìniànpǐn 纪念品 souvenir
jǐnjí chūkǒu 紧急出口 emergency exit
jìnkǒu 进口 import, to import, entrance
jīntiān 今天 today
jīntiān wǎnshàng 今天晚上 tonight
jīntiān xiàwǔ 今天下午 this afternoon
jīntiān zǎoshàng 今天早上 this morning
jiùmìng 救命 Help!
jiùshēngtǐng 救生艇 lifeboat
jiùshēngyī 救生衣 lifejacket
jízhěn 急诊 emergency *(in hospital)*
júgōng 鞠躬 to bow
jùyuàn 剧院 theatre

K

kāfēi 咖啡 coffee
kāi shuǐ 开水 boiling/boiled water
kāichē 开车 to depart
kǎpiàn 卡片 cards
kè 课 lesson
kě 渴 thirsty
kējì 科技 technology
kèrén 客人 guest
kēxué 科学 science
kēxuéjiā 科学家 scientist
kěyǐchīde 可以吃的 edible
kōng 空 empty
kòng fángjiān 空房间 vacancy *(at hotel)*
kòngquē 空缺 vacancy *(job)*
kōngtiáo 空调 air-conditioning
kǒuxiāng táng 口香糖 chewing gum
kòuzi 扣子 button
kǒuzi 口子 cut *(wound)*
kuài cān 快餐 fast food
kuàizi 筷子 chopsticks
kùzi 裤子 trousers

L

là 蜡 wax
là 辣 spicy
làjiāo/làzi 辣椒/辣子 chilli
lāliàn 拉链 zip
lán sè 蓝色 blue
lǎo 老 tough *(meat)*

lǎo yīdiǎn 老一点 well-done *(meat)*
láodòngbù 劳动布 denim
láojià 劳驾 excuse me
lǎoshī 老师 teacher
làzhú 蜡烛 candle
léi 雷 thunder
lèi 累 tired
lěng 冷 cold
lián wǎng 联网 internet connection
liǎngcì 两次 twice
lìjí 立即 immediately
lǐjiě 理解 understanding
líkāi 离开 to leave, to depart
lín shí 临时 temporary
líng 零 zero
lǐngdài 领带 tie
línghuó 灵活 flexible
língqián 零钱 change *(coin)*
lìngrén mǎnyìde 令人满意的 satisfactory
lìngrén shīwàng de 令人失望的 disappointing
lǐngshìguǎn 领事馆 consulate
línyù 淋浴 shower *(wash)*
lìshǐ 历史 history
liúlì 流利 fluent *(language)*
lǐwù 礼物 gift
lìxí 利息 interest *(bank)*
lìzhī 荔枝 lychee
lóng 聋 deaf
lóushàng 楼上 upstairs
lóutī 楼梯 stairs
lóuxià 楼下 downstairs
lù 路 road
lù 鹿 deer
lùbiāo 路标 signpost
lún dào wǒ le 轮到我了 it's my turn
lùndiǎn 论点 argument
lúnyǐ 轮椅 wheelchair
lúnzi 轮子 wheel
lǜsè 绿色 green
lǜshī 律师 solicitor, lawyer
lùtú 路途 journey, trip
lùxiàn 路线 route
lǚxíng rìchéng 旅行日程 itinerary
lǚxíng shè 旅行社 travel agent
lǚyóu 旅游 to travel
lǚyóu chē 旅游车 tourist coach

M

mài 卖 to sell
mǎi 买 to buy
mài guāng 卖光 sold-out
mǎidōngxī 买东西 shopping
máiyuàn 埋怨 complaint
màn 慢 slow, slowly
máng 忙 busy
mángrén 盲人 blind *(person)*
māo 猫 cat
máojīn 毛巾 towel
máopí 毛皮 fur
měi 美 beautiful
měi guó 美国 United States
méi lǐmào 没礼貌 impolite, rude
méi yìsī 没意思 boring
měi, měige 每，每个 every, each
méidiànle 没电了 flat *(battery)*
měige dìfāng 每个地方 everywhere
měigerén 每个人 everyone
měiguórén 美国人 American *(people)*
měitiān 每天 daily
měiyuán 美元 US dollar
měizhōu yīcìde 每周一次的 weekly
mí 迷 fan *(supporter)*

mǐ jiǔ 米酒 **rice wine**
miǎn fèi 免费 **free of charge**
miǎn shuì 免税 **duty-free**
miànbāo 面包 **bread**
miánhuāqiú 棉花球 **cotton wool**
miànjīnzhǐ 面巾纸 **tissues**
miànshì 面试 **interview, to interview**
miào 庙 **temple**
mǐfàn 米饭 **rice**
míngpiàn 名片 **business card**
míngrén 名人 **celebrity**
mìshū 秘书 **secretary**
mìyuè 蜜月 **honeymoon**
mòshuǐ 墨水 **ink**
mùtàn 木炭 **charcoal**
mùtóu 木头 **wood**

N

nà 那 **that** (demonstrative pronoun)
nàge 那个 **that** (pronoun)
nǎge 哪个 **which**
nán 南 **south**
nán 难 **hard, difficult**
nán péngyǒu 男朋友 **boyfriend**
nán tóngxìngliàn 男同性恋 **gay**
nàozhōng 闹钟 **alarm clock**
nàr 那儿 **there**
nǎr 哪儿 **where**
nǐ hǎo 你好 **hello**
nián 年 **year**
niàn 念 **to read**
niánlíng 年龄 **age**
niánqīng 年轻 **young**
niào 尿 **urine**
niǎo 鸟 **bird**
nǐde 你的 **your, yours** (singular)
nǐmen 你们 **you** (plural)
nǐmende 你们的 **your, yours** (plural)
niǔshāngle 扭伤了 **sprained**
nóng 浓 **strong** *(taste)*
nòng duàn 弄断 **to break**
nóngchǎng 农场 **farm**
nóngchǎngzhǔ 农场主 **farmer**
nóngcūn 农村 **countryside**
nònghuài 弄坏 **to damage**
nóngyè 农业 **agriculture**
nǚ cèsuǒ 女厕所 **women's toilet**
nǚ péngyou 女朋友 **girlfriend**
nǚ tóngxìngliàn zhě 女同性恋者 **lesbian**
nǚ zhǔrén 女主人 **hostess**
nuǎnhé 暖和 **warm** *(weather)*
nuǎnqì 暖气 **radiator, heating**
nǚcèsuǒ 女厕所 **ladies**
nǚde, nǚrén 女的，女人 **woman, women, female**
nǚér 女儿 **daughter**
nǚhái 女孩 **girl**
nǚhuáng 女皇 **empress**
nǚquán zhǔyìzhě 女权主义者 **feminist**

O

ǒutǔ 呕吐 **to vomit, be sick**
ōuyuán 欧元 **Euro**
ōuzhōu 欧洲 **Europe**

P

pāi zhào 拍照 **to take a photograph**
piàn 骗 **to cheat**
piānpì 偏僻 **remote**
piányí 便宜 **cheap**
piào 票 **ticket**
piào fáng 票房 **box office**

pígé 皮革 leather
pīn 拼 to spell *(a word)*
pīngpīng qiú 乒乓球 table tennis
píngzi 瓶子 bottle
pùbù 瀑布 waterfall

Q

qí 骑 to ride *(bycicle)*
qiān 千 thousand
qiánbāo 钱包 wallet
qiǎng 抢 to rob
qiāng 枪 gun
qiāngbì 枪毙 to execute
qiángjiān 强奸 to rape
qiǎngjié 抢劫 robbery
qiángyìng 强硬 firm *(tough)*
qiānmíng, qiānzì 签名, 签字 to sign, signature
qiánshuǐ 潜水 to dive
qiánshuǐ xīqì guǎn 潜水吸气管 snorkel
qiánshuǐde 潜水的 diving
qiántái 前台 reception *(in hotel)*
qiānzhèng 签证 visa
qiáo 桥 bridge
qiāoqiao shuō 悄悄说 to whisper
qíchē rén 骑车人 cyclist
qǐng zhèbiān zǒu 请这边走 this way, please
qǔ xiāo 取消 to cancel
quánqiúxìng biànnuǎn 全球性变暖 global warming
quánshuǐ 泉水 fountain
quèshí 确实 indeed, exactly
qúnzi 裙子 skirt

R

rè 热 hot *(weather)*
rěng diào 扔掉 to throw away
rènhé dìfāng 任何地方 anywhere
rènhéshì 任何事 anything
rénzàode 人造的 artificial, synthetic
rèqì 热气 heat
rèqíng 热情 enthusiastic
rìběn 日本 Japan
rìběnrén 日本人 Japanese *(people)*
rìcháng yǐnshí 日常饮食 diet
rìchéng 日程 schedule
rìchū 日出 sunrise
rìjì 日记 diary
rìlì 日历 calendar
rìqī 日期 date
rìwén 日文 Japanese *(language)*
róngyì 容易 easy
ruǎn yǐnliào 软饮料 soft drinks
ruǎnjiàn 软件 software
rùchǎng 入场 admission *(to a park)*
rùkǒu 入口 entrance
ruò 弱 weak *(person)*

S

sài mǎ 赛马 horse racing
shàitàiyáng 晒太阳 to sunbathe
shǎizi 骰子 dice
shǎndiàn 闪电 lightening
shāndòng 山洞 cave
shàngdì 上帝 God
shāngdiàn 商店 shop
shāngkǒu 伤口 wound
shāngpǐn jiāoyìhuì 商品交易会 trade fair
shāngrén 商人 businessman, businesswoman

shāngǔ 山谷 **valley**
shǎnguāngdēng 闪光灯 **flash** *(for camera)*
shàngxiàbān shíjiān 上下班时间 **rush hour**
shāngyè zhōngxīn 商业中心 **shopping centre**
shàngyī 上衣 **jacket**
sháozi 勺子 **spoon**
shéi 谁 **who**
shéide 谁的 **whose**
shèngdànjié 圣诞节 **Christmas**
shēngjiāng 生姜 **ginger**
shèngjīng 圣经 **Bible**
shēngqì 生气 **to be cross, annoyed**
shěngqiánde 省钱的 **economical, money-saving**
shēngrén 生人 **stranger**
shēngrì 生日 **birthday**
shēngyì 生意 **business**
shénme 什么 **what**
shénme shíhòu 什么时候 **when**
shēnshì 绅士 **gentleman**
shēntǐ 身体 **health**
shēnzi 身子 **body**
shèshī 设施 **facilities**
shī wù 失物 **lost property**
shìde 是的 **yes**
shìgù 事故 **accident**
shíkèbiǎo 时刻表 **timetable**
shíwù zhòngdú 食物中毒 **food poisoning**
shìyàng 式样 **style** *(clothing)*
shīyè 失业 **unemployed**
shǒubiǎo 手表 **watch**
shǒudū 首都 **capital** *(city)*
shōufèi 收费 **to charge** *(money)*
shǒugōng zuòde 手工做的 **handmade**
shòuhuò yuán 售货员 **shop-assistant**
shōujù 收据 **receipt**
shǒujuàn 手绢 **handkerchief**
shōukuǎnrén 收款人 **cashier**
shòupiào chǔ 售票处 **ticket office**
shǒutí dài 手提袋 **carrier bag**
shǒutí diànnǎo 手提电脑 **laptop**
shǒutí xínglǐ 手提行李 **hand luggage**
shǒutí xiāng 手提箱 **briefcase, suitcase**
shǒutíbāo 手提包 **handbag**
shōuxià 收下 **to accept** *(present)*
shōuyǎng 收养 **to adopt** *(children)*
shōuyǎngde 收养的 **adopted**
shǒuzhuó 手镯 **bracelet**
shǔ 数 **to count**
shū 书 **book**
shuā 刷 **to brush**
shuāngrén chuáng 双人床 **double bed**
shūfǎ 书法 **calligraphy**
shuǐ 水 **water**
shuǐguǒ 水果 **fruit**
shuǐguǒtáng 水果糖 **sweets**
shuìshōu 税收 **tax**
shùmǎ 数码 **digital**
sǐ 死 **to die, dead**
sīchóu 丝绸 **silk**
sījī 司机 **driver**
sīkāi 撕开 **to tear** *(to rip)*
SIM kǎ SIM 卡 **SIM card**
sòngdú kùnnán de 诵读困难的 **dyslexic**
sù cài/sù shí 素菜/素食 **vegetarian food**
sù zuì 宿醉 **hangover**

sùdù xiànzhì 速度限制 speed limit
sūgélán 苏格兰 Scotland
sūgélánrén 苏格兰人 Scottish *(people)*

T

tā 她 she
tā 他 he, him
tā 它 it
tāde 她的 her, hers
tāde 他的 his
tài 太 too *(extremely)*
tàibàngle 太棒了 fantastic
tàiguó 泰国 Thailand
táijiē 台阶 terrace
tàitai 太太 Mrs, wife
tàiyáng 太阳 sun
tàiyáng yǎnjìng 太阳眼镜 sunglasses
tāmen 他们 they, them
tāmende 他们的 their, theirs
tān 摊 stall, stand
tǎng xià 躺下 to lie down
tángniàobìng 糖尿病 diabetes
tánhuà 谈话 conversation
tǎnzi 毯子 blanket
tào cān 套餐 set menu
táocí 陶瓷 ceramics
tèbié 特别 special
tiānqì 天气 weather
tiānqì yùbào 天气预报 weather forecast
tìhú dāo, tìxū dāo 剃胡刀, 剃须刀 razor
tíqián 提前 in advance
tōuláide 偷来的 stolen
tuìxiūle 退休了 retired
tūn 吞 to swallow
tuō yīfú 脱衣服 to undress
túzhāng 图章 seal *(name stamp)*

U

U pán liánxiàn U盘联线 USB lead

W

wàiguórén 外国人 foreigner
wàijiāo shìwù 外交事务 foreign affairs
wàijiāoguān 外交官 diplomat
wǎn 晚 late
wǎn 碗 bowl, dish
wǎn'ān 晚安 good night
wǎncān 晚餐 dinner
wǎngluò 网络 web *(internet)*
wǎngluò shèjìzhě 网络设计者 web designer
wǎngqiú 网球 tennis
wǎngqiú chǎng 网球场 tennis court
wàngyuǎnjìng 望远镜 binoculars
wánjù 玩具 toy
wǎnshàng 晚上 evening
wǎnshàng hǎo 晚上好 good evening
wèidào 味道 taste, flavour
wèir 味儿 smell
wēi'ěrshì 威尔士 Wales
wēi'ěrshìrén 威尔士人 Welsh *(people)*
wèihūnfū 未婚夫 fiancé
wèihūnqī 未婚妻 fiancée
wéijīn 围巾 scarf
wéile 为了 for
wéimiào 微妙 delicate *(matter)*
wèishēng jiān 卫生间 bathroom
wèishēng jīn 卫生巾 sanitary towel
wèishēng yòngpǐn 卫生用品 toiletries

wèishēng zhǐ 卫生纸 toilet paper
wéishēngsù 维生素 vitamin
wéishénme 为什么 why
wēishìjì 威士忌 whisky
wéixiǎnde 危险的 dangerous
wéixiào 微笑 smile
wéizuǐ 围嘴 bib
wèn 问 to ask
wénhuà 文化 culture
wénjiàn 文件 file, document
wǒ 我 I, me
wò shǒu 握手 to shake hands
wǒmen 我们 we, us
wǔrǔ 侮辱 to insult

X

xī 西 west
xī cān 西餐 western food
xī shì 西式 western-style
xǐ'àide 喜爱的 favourite (adj.)
xià yǔ 下雨 to rain
xián 咸 salty
xiāng gǎng 香港 Hong Kong
xiǎng jiā 想家 to be homesick
xiàngqí 象棋 chess
xiàngyá 象牙 ivory
xiāngyān 香烟 cigarette
xiànjīn 现金 cash
xiānjìn 先进 advanced *(technology)*
xiánliáo 闲聊 to chat, to gossip
xiànmù 羡慕 to admire
xiānshēng 先生 sir, Mr, husband
xiāochuǎn 哮喘 asthma
xiǎofèi 小费 tip
xiǎohái 小孩 child, children
xiàohuà 笑话 joke
xiǎoshēng shuō 小声说 to whisper
xiǎoshí 小时 hour
xiāoyán 消炎 antiseptic
xiǎoyuèduì 小乐队 band *(music)*
xiǎozǔ 小组 team, group
xiàwǔ 下午 afternoon
xiàxuě 下雪 to snow
xiàzài 下载 to download
xīdú zhě 吸毒者 drug addict
xiě 写 to write
xiě 血 blood
xiě xíng 血型 blood type
xièxie 谢谢 thanks, thank you
xīfāngde 西方的 western
xǐhuān 喜欢 to like, to enjoy
xíjí 袭击 to attack
xìn yòng kǎ 信用卡 credit card
xìnfēng 信封 envelope
xíng 行 all right
xìng 性 sex
xìng 姓 surname, family name
xínglǐ 行李 luggage, baggage
xīnjiāpō 新加坡 Singapore
xìnxí 信息 information
xīnxiān 新鲜 fresh
xǐyīfáng 洗衣房 laundry
xīyǒu 稀有 rare
xīzàng 西藏 Tibet
xǐzǎo 洗澡 bath
xuǎnjǔ 选举 election
xué 学 to learn
xuěbēng 雪崩 avalanche
xuéqī 学期 term *(school)*
xuéshēng 学生 student
xuéwèi 学位 university degree
xuéxí 学习 to study
xuéxiào 学校 school
xuéyuàn 学院 college

xùjiǔ de rén 酗酒的人 alcoholic *(person)*
xūruò 虚弱 fragile

Y

yángé sùshízhě 严格素食者 vegan
yànhuǒ 焰火 firework
yǎnjìng 眼镜 spectacles, glasses
yánjiùshēng 研究生 graduate *(student)*
yáqiān 牙签 toothpick
yīcìxìng 一次性 disposable
yīduìr 一对儿 a couple *(a pair)*
yín 银 silver
yīng'ér 婴儿 baby
yīng'ér nǎipíng 婴儿奶瓶 baby's bottle
yīngbàng 英镑 sterling
yìngbì 硬币 coin
yīng'ér chuáng 婴儿床 cot
yīnggélán 英格兰 England
yīngguó 英国 Britain
yīngguórén 英国人 British *(people)*
yīngtáo 樱桃 cherry
yīngyǔ 英语 English *(language)*
yínháng 银行 bank
yǐnyòngshuǐ 饮用水 drinking water
yīnyuè dàtīng 音乐大厅 concert hall
yīnyuèhuì 音乐会 concert
yīqǐ 一起 together
yīqiē 一切 everything
yīqúnrén 一群人 crowd
yīshēng 医生 doctor
yìshù 艺术 art
yìshùjiā 艺术家 artist
yīsīlán 伊斯兰 Islam
yīsīlán jiàode 伊斯兰教的 Islamic
yīwùsuǒ 医务所 clinic
yīxiē 一些 some
yīyàng 一样 same
yīyuàn 医院 hospital
yōngjǐ 拥挤 crowded
yòu'ér gāo yǐzi 幼儿高椅子 high chair
yǒuhǎode 友好的 friendly
yóukè 游客 tourist
yǒumíng 有名 famous
yōumò 幽默 humour
yóupiào 邮票 stamps
yóutài jiàotáng 犹太教堂 synagogue
yóutàijiào de dàshī 犹太教的大师 rabbi
yóutàirén 犹太人 Jewish
yǒuxiào 有效 valid *(ticket)*
yóuxíng 游行 demonstration
yóuyǒng chí 游泳池 swimming pool
yóuyǒng yǎnjìng 游泳眼镜 goggles
yóuyǒng yī 游泳衣 swimming trunks, swimsuit
yù 玉 jade
yuán 元 yuan *(Chinese currency)*
yùdìng 预订 reservation, to reserve
yùdìngde 预订的 reserved
yuēhuì 约会 appointment
yuèjīng miánsāi 月经棉塞 tampons
yǔfǎ 语法 grammar
yùjīn 浴巾 bath towel
yūn chē, yūn chuán, yūn jī 晕车，晕船，晕机 travel sickness
yūnchuán 晕船 seasick
yùnqìhǎo 运气好 lucky

Z

zài....dǐxià 在....底下 under
zài...pángbiān 在...旁边 beside

zài...shàng 在..... 上 above
zài...yǐwài 在...以外 beyond
zài...zhījiān 在.... 之间 between
zài...zhīqián 在...之前 by the end of
zài...lǐmiàn 在...里面 inside
zài...qījiān 在...期间 during
zàijiàn 再见 goodbye
zàng 脏 dirty
zànglǐ 葬礼 funeral
zǎo 早 early
zǎofàn 早饭 breakfast
zǎoshàng hǎo 早上好 good morning
zhāodàihuì 招待会 reception *(welcome party)*
zhàoxiàngjī 照相机 camera
zhāpí 扎啤 draught beer
zhē 蜇 to sting
zhè shìhé nǐ 这适合你 it suits you
zhèr 这儿 here
zhège xīngqī 这个星期 this week
zhège yuè 这个月 this month
zhēn kěxí 真可惜 shame: what a shame!
zhèngfǔ 政府 government
zhèngshì 正式 formal
zhèngshū 证书 certificate
zhēnjiǔ 针灸 acupuncture
zhī 汁 juice
zhīdào 知道 to know
zhíde 值得 worth
zhìdù 制度 system
zhīmá 芝麻 sesame
zhìmìng 致命 fatal
zhòng 重 heavy
zhōngdiǎn 终点 destination
zhōngguó 中国 China
zhōngguórén 中国人 Chinese *(people)*
zhōngwén 中文 Chinese *(language)*
zhōng yào 中药 Chinese medicine
zhōng yī 中医 traditional Chinese medicine doctor
zhōu 州 state *(in USA)*
zhōumò 周末 weekend
zhōunián 周年 anniversary
zhùjiǔ 祝酒 to have a toast
zhǔrén 主人 host
zhùshǒu 助手 assistant
zhùsù 住宿 accommodation
zhǔxí 主席 chairman
zhǔyì 主意 idea
zhúzi 竹子 bamboo
zhùzuǐ 住嘴 shut up!
zì 字 Chinese character
zìxíngchē zūlìn 自行车租赁 bicycle for hire
zì zhù 自助 self-service
zǐcài 紫菜 seaweed *(edible)*
zìdiǎn 字典 dictionary
zǒngbù 总部 headquarters
zōngjiào 宗教 religion
zǒngshì 总是 always
zǒngshù 总数 total
zuì 醉 drunk
zuò de búcuò 做得不错 well done)
zuò fàn 做饭 to cook
zuòjiā 作家 writer, author
zuòqūjiā 作曲家 composer
zuótiān 昨天 yesterday
zuòwéi 作为 as
zuòwèi 座位 seat
zuǒyòu 左右 about, approximately
zúqiú 足球 football, soccer